30.00
70C

AAK-8862

D0207987

WITHDRAWN

The Teacher

Philosophy of Education Research Library

Series editors
  V. A. Howard and Israel Scheffler
  Harvard Graduate School of Education

Already published

The Teacher

Theory and Practice in Teacher Education

Allen T. Pearson

Routledge

New York   London

To the memory of my parents

First published in 1989 by
Routledge
an imprint of Routledge, Chapman & Hall, Inc.
29 West 35th Street
New York NY 10001

Published in Great Britain by
Routledge
11 New Fetter Lane
London EC4P 4EE

© 1989 by Allen T. Pearson

Printed in the United States of America

All rights reserved. No part of this book may be
reprinted or reproduced or utilized in any form or
by any electronic, mechanical, or other means, now
known or hereafter invented, including photocopying
and recording, or in any information storage or
retrieval system, without permission in writing
from the publishers.

Library of Congress Cataloging in Publication Data

Pearson, Allen T., 1944-
  The teacher: theory and practice in teacher education / Allen T.
Pearson.
    p.   cm.—(Philosophy of education research library)
  Bibliography: p.
  Includes index.
  ISBN 0-415-90088-3
  1. Teachers—Training of. 2.Teaching. I. Title.
LB1707.P42 1989   89-10333
370′.71—dc20

British Library Cataloguing in Publication Data
also available

Contents

Preface

In 1980 the Dean of my Faculty of Education appointed a philosopher of education to the position of Assistant Dean (Practicum), the position called in many other universities the Director of Student Teaching. No one, at least in my hearing, ever suggested that this was an odd or unusual appointment to make, though I am sure some wondered. It was for me, however, the beginning of a fascinating time in my life; I had to come to grips with ideas and issues that I had not had to face, and I had the opportunity to work with many dedicated and insightful people from fields, perspectives and backgrounds other than my own. One of the topics I found myself discussing in this position was the importance of integrating theory and practice in teacher education. I defended my Faculty to the teachers, superintendents and executive staff of the teacher's association and government officials on the grounds that our program did indeed integrate theory and practice. These were essentially political defenses about which I never felt entirely comfortable. Upon leaving this position and returning to my usual responsibilities as a philosopher of education I decided that I would try to make some philosophical sense of what I had been talking about for four years. The present work is the result of my endeavors.

I owe thanks to many for their assistance in helping to educate me in matters of teacher education. I wish especially to express my thanks to Walter Worth, the Dean who appointed me to the student teaching position, for giving me the opportunity to participate in this vital area. My colleagues on the Faculty of Education taught me much, and their patience with me was remarkable. The members of the Teacher Education and Certification Committee of the Alberta Teachers' Association gave me, during my tenure on that committee, a crash course in the issues of teacher education as seen from the teacher's viewpoint. They may not agree with all that I say; but they have profoundly influenced what I have to say. I wish also to thank Eamonn Callan for many suggestions and Leela Kobbekaduwa for much help in preparing the manuscript.

When I first left my student teaching responsibilities I was fortunate to be able to be a Visiting Fellow at the Philosophy of Education Research Center at Harvard University. I wish to thank its co-directors, Israel Scheffler and Vernon Howard, for their hospitality and the encouragement they gave me to turn my initial reflections on the question of theory and practice into this book.

CHAPTER 1

Introduction

Questions and problems of education soon become questions and problems of teacher education. It is not uncommon, and it is certainly understandable, that we turn our attention to the preparation of teachers when we are concerned with the education of the young and with the quality of the schools. When we begin to look at teacher education the issue of "theory and practice" begins to loom large. That this should have become a catch phrase in education stems no doubt from the way we have conceived teacher education. It is almost a universal feature of teacher education programs that they contain four components: general education, specialized knowledge, professional knowledge and practice.[1] Given that these components mean to provide the intending teacher with the knowledge and capabilities to become a professional teacher, teacher education expects the intending teacher to take the knowledge presented, which is often theoretical, and to apply it in classroom practice. It is this expectation, which is suggested by the label "the relation of theory and practice," that is my topic in this work.

My intention is to treat this topic as a philosophical one. My concern is to provide a conceptual understanding of theory and practice and their alleged relation. This endeavor is made difficult by the range of meanings that have been given to theory and practice in the literature. Sometimes one finds theory and practice identified, or seemingly identified, with what goes on in universities and what goes on in schools: "The three commonplaces of teacher education—the dichotomy of theory (university instruction) and practice (schooling)."[2] At the other extreme we find difficult and sophisticated discussions of how theory and practice can be integrated and even be made identical.[3] Neither of these positions seems plausible. Surely, in the first case, theoretical matters can be found in schools and practical matters in universities. In the second case, one wants to say an integration or amalgamation of what is theoretical and what is practical is to remove an important basis for distinguishing ideas and activities. Admittedly it is often difficult to distinguish between the theoretical and practical and what counts as theoretical in one context may well count as practical in another. In spite of the difficulties inherent in these notions, they do seem to be ones that we do not want to lose. The question, then, that I want to consider here from a philosophical point of view, is what is the most plausible and fruitful way of conceptualizing the relation between theory and practice.

I will attempt to answer this question in two ways. First, I will consider and criticize some of the answers that have been given. Second, I will develop an alternative position that is not subject to the criticisms I will lay against the other accounts of theory and practice. The positions I will consider fall in two groups. The first set of positions see theory as being essentially scientific and practice as applied science. In the philosophy of education literature, a basic starting point for discussions of theory and practice is the debate between D. J. O'Connor and P. H. Hirst[4] on the nature of educational theory. In Chapter 2 I will consider O'Connor's position in this debate. He defends the view that theory in education should be considered in the same way that it is considered in the natural and social sciences. This view will receive, in terms of space I devote to the topic, my greatest attention. It seems to me that this view is the one reflected most clearly in contemporary educational research. Because of its widespread acceptance I will need to spend some extra time with it. More controversially, I shall, in Chapter 3, consider the work of Donald Schön as an example of an account of theory and practice that is essentially scientific. His work is extremely insightful and provocative but, I will want to claim, not entirely acceptable. Although Schön claims to be developing an alternative epistemology to "technical rationality," I will try to show that his position falls within the general class of scientific approaches to an understanding of theory and practice; that is, his work is not as different as he claims, even though it adds much to our understanding of this issue.

After this consideration of scientific views of theory and practice, I will consider two approaches that put the basis for understanding educational theory and practice in philosophy. The history of educational theory is, to a large degree, a story of a variety of accounts of the purposes, policies and practices of education that are essentially philosophical. From Plato through Comenius, Locke and many others to present day thinkers, educational theory has been taken by many to be an essentially philosophical enterprise. That it might be a scientific activity is only a recent development.

The first of these positions to be examined, in Chapter 4, is Hirst's side of his debate with O'Connor. This position, which I call a "normative" theory of education, conceives of educational theory as a multidisciplinary theory drawing on the social sciences, philosophy, ethics and experience. The second position is Donna Kerr's conception of a "theory of practice." This view, discussed in Chapter 5, elucidates the concepts of theory and practice in the context of action theory, a philosophical account of how human action is to be understood.

In my discussion of these four positions, I will raise a number of questions and criticisms, but they all, I feel, have something to contribute to the final position that I will develop. This is done principally in Chapters 6 and 7. Chapter 6 may appear to be a detour; in that chapter

I will discuss teaching and what, from a philosophical point of view, it entails. I do this because the account of theory and practice that I want to present is based on the practice of teaching. Part of my position is that our understanding of theory and practice in teaching should grow out of our understanding of teaching, not from some prior commitments as to the nature of theory and practice. In discussing teaching I can make clear the nature of its practice, so that in Chapter 7 I can discuss how theory and practice can plausibly be understood in education.

In that chapter I will refocus the question of theory and practice. I will try to show that the concern we have for relating theory and practice is the concern for how teachers utilize the knowledge and beliefs they have. The fundamental issue behind the question of theory and practice, I will claim, is the relation between belief and action. I will present an account of how belief and action are related through the reasoning that teachers engage in. How teachers use what they know and believe in deciding what to do is, I want to claim, the essential issue behind the catch phrase, "relating theory to practice." My view, instead of locating this discussion in a predetermined scientific or philosophical account of theory, claims that it is based in the reasoning that teachers do as part of their daily life and work. The thesis that I will be presenting and defending in this work, then, is that the concern for relating theory and practice in education is met when teachers use their knowledge and beliefs to make reasonable and reasoned decisions about what to do in their classrooms.

By this point I hope to have established that my thesis is plausible. In Chapter 8 I try to show that my thesis is fruitful. In this chapter I try to draw the implications of the thesis for teacher education. If translating theory into practice involves making reasoned decisions about what to do given one's knowledge and beliefs then teacher education will need to prepare intending teachers for making these decisions. I try to suggest what a teacher education program that takes this position seriously would need to contain. Finally, I will use the thesis to show how it helps us to understand and evaluate some of the proposals for teacher education that are currently in vogue.

The upshot of this discussion is, I hope, to show that our thinking about teacher education needs to and can benefit from careful philosophical study. Those who are entrusted with the education of the young of any society are given a task of the greatest importance and consequence. Those who are involved in the preparation and education of those teachers are engaged in a task of no less importance. Such a task deserves our most careful study and attention, whether we approach the task from philosophical or scientific standpoints; the education of teachers demands no less. Whether or not my thesis is judged to be correct, I hope that what I have to say will be provocative enough to encourage further philosophical investigations into the grounds of teacher education.

CHAPTER 2

Practice as applied science

In investigating the relation of theory and practice in teacher education, a first approximation of how the two notions are to be understood is to liken the relation to that found in the practice of medicine. There, clearly, the theory is that found in the biological sciences, and practice is found in the interaction between the physician and the patient. It seems obvious that the practice of medicine is guided by the theoretical knowledge of the physician. Physicians take the theoretical knowledge that they possess as a result of their education and apply it to a particular case at hand. The education of the physician is, then, an effort to provide the student with general knowledge of the field that can be applied in the everyday practice of medicine. While I would not want to push this analogy too far, and indeed I will return to it to discuss its limitations, it is a forceful analogy that one commonly finds in discussions about the relation of theory and practice in education. The force of the analogy is in no small part due to the success of medicine. The biological sciences have provided the practice of medicine with much knowledge and many treatments that can be used in the care of individual people. One author who has used the view behind this analogy as a basis for conceptualizing educational theory, while recognizing its limitations, is D. J. O'Connor.[1] I will turn first to his view of educational theory.

Educational theory is scientific

Given the vagueness of the word "theory" and the many different contexts in which it can be used, O'Connor's approach is to offer a stipulative definition which tries to capture the basic idea behind the notion of a scientific theory and to defend it against objections. It is: a theory is "a logically interrelated set of hypotheses confirmed by observation and which has the further properties of being both refutable and explanatory."[2] He spends some time discussing the notions of being refutable and explanatory, but does not discuss the notion of being confirmed by observation. The latter notion, though, is important. It makes clear that a theory, and consequently an educational theory, is a set of inductive, empirical statements. Only those statements that are confirmable by observation are candidates for inclusion in an educational theory. This, it almost goes without saying, rules out many of the kinds of claims we find in education from being part of a theory of education.

Normative claims and many of the policy claims that govern the operation of educational institutions are not confirmable by observation, at least not in any obvious sense. To claim that handicapped children should receive the same educational opportunities as the non-handicapped or that every child should learn how to operate a computer are not the kinds of claims that one can confirm by observation. Although what one observes has a bearing upon whether these claims should be adopted, this would seem to be insufficient for their adoption. One also has to make judgments about the principles on which these claims rest or on the consequences of so acting. So, while it is a commonplace of conceptualizations about scientific theory that they include only those claims that are based on observation, it is a view that has important ramifications for the conceptualization of educational theory.

The other two criteria in the definition, what he calls his "minimal criteria," need some clarification. He adopts the "deductive" model of explanation. His view, again a commonplace in accounts of scientific explanation, is that an event is explained when a statement of that event can be deduced from other true statements, at least one of which is a statement of a general law of science. For us to know that the statement explains an event we need to know, under this model of explanation, that certain general laws and statements of initial conditions are true, and that the statement in question can be derived from the other statements in the explanation in accordance with the rules of logic.

The second criterion, refutability, rules out of scientific theories those claims and sets of claims that are impervious to test or experiment. Some sorts of claims are such that although they have confirming instances there is no possibility that they can be disconfirmed. Such claims are not suitable candidates for inclusion in a scientific theory. Astrology is a common example of a non-refutable set of claims. Apparent counter-evidence is never, in astrology, treated as threatening the truth of the claims themselves; the disconfirming instances can always be explained away. Here the vagueness of the claims and their ability to be interpreted in a variety of ways are what make them non-refutable. Other more debatable examples of non-refutable sets of claims that masquerade as science, but examples which O'Connor accepts as clear cases of non-refutable sets of claims, are psychoanalysis and Marxism.

So, the view of theory under consideration is the standard, even doctrinal, view of science. A theory is a set of statements that explain particular events by reference to general laws. These laws are based, ultimately, on observation, and the theory is itself always open to modification or refutation. This view of science has become so common that it may almost seem a caricature. But if educational theory can be construed in this way we have a very powerful position. All the credibility that accrues to science will accrue to education, and practitioners of education will have a strong and secure base on which to base their actions.

Limitations of the position

In adopting this position, O'Connor recognizes that it has what might be called limitations. The first has already been mentioned in that a theory of education conceptualized in this manner will not include value or normative claims. The field of education is one, however, in which normative claims are prominent; the very first questions that must be asked in education—why should we educate children, what should we teach them, and who should be taught—all raise difficult normative issues. Until they are answered, the factual questions concerning the organization and procedures of education cannot be considered. So, it would seem, that a conceptualization of educational theory that ignores such issues must be defective.

This conclusion is too hasty. Normative claims can guide the practice of education without being part of educational theory. The analogy of medicine can be appealed to again. Values concerning health, the absence of disease and access to medical care can guide the practice of the physician even though these issues do not appear in the scientific underpinnings of medicine. Similarly, in education the normative questions can be considered and answered independently of theoretical questions. Once positions have been developed about why we should educate, what should be taught, and the like, the results can be used to guide practice. The fact that normative issues are not part of an educational theory does not mean that they are considered irrelevant to the practice of education. They can guide practice from outside the theory.

This leads to a conclusion that O'Connor does not recognize. Given this conception of theory, it is now clear that a theory of education is at best necessary, but not sufficient, for the direction of practice. Since the normative claims of education are outside the theory of education and since normative claims are needed for guiding the practice of education, an educational theory is not alone sufficient for guiding practice. No matter how well developed our theory of education is, it will not by itself be able to direct the practice of education. We will always need, at least, a normative position that will help to direct the actions that one pursues.

Further, and what O'Connor does see, an educational theory is not necessary for the practice of education.[3] The practice of education was not only established, but was quite effective, before there was any scientific theory of education. So given that the practice can be quite sophisticated without a theory of education, such a theory is not necessary for practice. What has made theory increasingly relevant to the practice of education, according to O'Connor, is the development of mass education. When education was restricted to a few, academically talented children, the practice of education did not need the resources of a theory of education to become more successful. The resources and experience of the teacher were sufficient. However, now that "the benefits of literacy and numeracy are such that no one must be spared them,"[4] the practice of education has become much more difficult. In having to teach everyone, regardless of talent, interest or ambition, the challenges to the teacher have become much greater. In order to meet these challenges, education has turned to psychology and sociology, in particular, for help.

This, according to O'Connor, is one place where the analogy of education to medicine breaks down. The practice of education has developed to a large extent without the need for scientific theory. Education only turned to science when it reached the point where as a result of a social revolution it became unable to cope with the problems set before it. The practice of medicine, on the other hand, is the result of a scientific revolution. Medicine as we know it would not be possible except for developments in science. That is, the growth of science preceded and made possible developments in the field of medicine. Medicine did not develop and then turn to science for help and support as in the case of education. So, the relations between theory and practice are different in education and medicine.

Another limitation on the conceptualization of educational theory as scientific is the limited support the sciences are able to provide to the practice of education. It has often been noted that the practice of education is informed to a remarkably small extent by the sciences of psychology and sociology. The results of these sciences have little to say to the practitioners of education. In part this is due to the obvious nature of the findings. Educational theory seems more likely to reaffirm what the practitioner already realizes rather than to provide new information. The "time-on-task" studies tell us that students who spend more time learning a subject have greater success in learning that subject. Such a finding is not very startling, to say the least. Other sorts of findings of the educational sciences seem to have no bearing on educational practice because of their distance from the world of the practitioner. Studies of memory retention use the subject's ability to recall patterns of nonsense syllables. Since the actual practice of education is not concerned with learning nonsense, these studies have little bearing on the practice of education.[5]

A number of reasons can be identified for the lack of support that the social sciences have been able to provide for educational practice. One reason may stem from the point made above about medicine and education. Medicine has a history of a much closer and successful relation with its scientific base than education. But in medicine it has been the scientific disciplines that have set the agenda for medicine. The practice of medicine is a direct outgrowth of developments in the related sciences, and so it is not surprising that it should show a close and harmonious relation to those sciences. Education, on the other hand, has developed independently of the social sciences and has only turned to them in recent times because traditional practice has been forced to deal with new and difficult conditions. In education, the sciences have not set the agenda for the practice of education. Rather, the practice of education has sought to influence the agenda of independent scientific activities. So, it is again not surprising that there is not the close relation between the practice and the theory of education.

Two more standard answers to the question of why scientific theory has had so little to say to educational practice are first that the sciences of psychology and sociology are young and immature, and second that the idea of a social science is misconceived. The first answer is the one appealed to by O'Connor, among others. The claim here is that in the history of science, psychology and sociology are relatively young; they have been in existence only for about a century. While we cannot be sure of their future development, we cannot say with any certainty that they will not provide support for education comparable to that provided by biology and chemistry to the practice of medicine. There is no basis for dismissing psychology and sociology as having nothing to say to education on the basis that to date they have had little, if anything, to say. A related point is the alleged obviousness of the findings of the social sciences. As humans, we exist in a social world and so develop some knowledge, albeit rough and ready, of what it is to be a social agent in the world. Since this is also the aim of the social sciences, it is not unexpected that the findings of social science should appear obvious. If our experience has any basis in reality then the results of the social sciences should be similar to our experience. But the social sciences do provide a sound scientific base for that knowledge in comparison to the personal and perhaps idiosyncratic base of one person's experience.

The second sort of answer to the question of why the social sciences have had so little to say to the practice of education is more radical. This is to say that the very notion of a social science is misconceived.[6] The study of human action, it is alleged, is not the kind of thing that can be done scientifically. To apply categories and procedures that have their home in the study of physical objects to the study of human beings is unwarranted. The kind of knowledge that we get from ordinary experience is sufficient for understanding humans and, indeed, is the only kind of knowledge that we can have of humans. In relation to the practice of education this line of argument means that it is inappropriate to turn to the sciences to provide guidance for what is to be done in schools. Rather, the kind of knowledge that one gets from experience in schools and education is the only kind of knowledge that one needs to guide practice. This debate, of course, must be returned to for more examination.

Criticisms of the position

I now want to turn to some fundamental issues that must be faced when educational theory is claimed to be scientific in the standard sense.

From the point of view of looking at this issue with the question of the relation of theory to practice in mind, this claim gets its plausibility from the success of other applications, in particular medicine, of the results of science to the realm of practice. If there are serious doubts about whether educational theory is scientific in the same way as, say, medical theory is, then the plausibility of the analogy begins to wane. I will consider some questions about the nature of educational theory as presented so far and will then turn to questions of the relation of educational theory conceived in this way to educational practice.

Under this view of educational theory, the content of the theory is provided by psychology and sociology alone. These are the realms of science that give descriptions and explanations of educational phenomena, or at least those that are amenable to scientific understanding. I have already pointed out that this conception excludes normative and policy issues from any putative educational theory. But the status of psychology and sociology as scientific, in the sense elucidated, is not without controversy. It has been argued that these fields are not sciences, or that insofar as they are sciences they have nothing of any interest to tell us.

To begin to face this issue I would first like to elucidate what I take to be two necessary conditions for being a social science. These are in addition to any conditions that must be met for something to be a science, conditions such as being explanatory and refutable. The two conditions that I have in mind are that a social science must include mental events as part of its content and that a social science must describe lawful events.

To consider the mental events condition first, a mental event is one that will be described by a sentence containing a verb which expresses a propositional attitude, or to put it in more technical language, "such verbs are characterized by the fact that they sometimes feature in sentences with subjects that refer to persons, and are completed by embedded sentences in which the usual rules of substitution appear to breakdown."[7] Mental events, then, would be such events as desiring something, believing something, intending something, and more pertinent for my purposes, learning something or knowing something. Such events are mental because the verbs in each case sometimes have a person as their subject and occur in sentences where the verbs are followed by embedded sentences in which the normal rules of substitution do not hold. For example, a person may learn that Jane Austen wrote *Northanger Abbey*. Suppose that it is true Austen is the only author buried in Winchester Cathedral, then the descriptions "the author of *Northanger Abbey*" and "the author buried in Winchester Cathedral" refer to the same person. The usual rules of substitution allow for the substitution of identities. But in this case, while it is true that the person has learned that Jane Austen wrote *Northanger Abbey,* it does not follow that it is true that the person has learned that Jane Austen is buried in Winchester Cathedral. So, the usual rules of substitution do not hold in embedded sentences that follow the verb "to learn," showing that this is an example of a mental verb. Similar considerations would show that this applies to all the other verbs that are of concern in education, such as "know," "believe," "understand," "appreciate," "value," and the like.

With this brief discussion of what is to count as a mental event, I want now to consider why social sciences must concern themselves with such events. The reason is quite simple. If an event is not mental, it is physical. So, if the social sciences were not concerned with mental events, they would be concerned only with physical events in which case there would be no difference between a social science and a physical science. That is to say, that which provides the possibility for the existence of a social science is the existence of mental events. Insofar as one is willing to allow the possibility of there being a social science one is committed to the claim that they must deal with mental events. The claim, then, that dealing with mental events is a necessary condition for being a social science can only be defeated by showing that physical sciences such as physiology and biology are sufficient to account for all human action. I take this claim to be implausible. Mental events can be described and explained without recourse to the concepts and theories of the biological sciences, and if such recourse is made, in general, it does not add to one's understanding of the mental event. So, if we accept that there are social sciences which are not equivalent or reducible to physical sciences we are committed to the claim that the social sciences must deal with mental events.

The position just set out does not state that the social sciences deal only with mental events. Physical events may well enter into a social science in order to account for, and to be accounted for by, mental events. In sociology, being born into a family of a certain social status is not a mental event, but is a relevant factor in a sociological explanation of a variety of mental events, such as what such a person believes or values. In psychology, the number of students in a classroom, a physical event, may influence what a person in that room learns, a mental event. So, a social science must include mental events, to provide the basis for differentiating it from physical sciences, but it need not include only mental events.

I now want to consider an argument from Davidson[8] which shows that a social science is not reducible or equivalent to natural science. One of the points that Davidson wants to establish is that there may be true statements linking the mental and the physical, but they are not lawlike[9] or, in other words, there are no strict psychophysical laws. Lawlikeness is a precondition for a scientific law. A statement is lawlike if it supports a subjunctive or counterfactual conditional, which is to say that "All A are B" is lawlike if it supports the claim that if something were to be an A it would be a B as well. But this condition is not sufficient; counter-examples can be constructed that show that supporting a subjunctive conditional is not enough to make a sentence lawlike. The predicate in the statement must be in some way suitable. Davidson wants to claim that mental predicates and physical predicates are "not made for one another" and so mental predicates are not suitable for physical events and vice versa. This is what establishes that true statements linking the mental and the physical are not lawlike.

What is the basis for claiming that mental and physical predicates are not made for one another? The difference, according to Davidson, lies in the commitments made in the mental and physical schemes.[10] A physical theory accounts for change within its own scheme. A change in the physical world can be described and explained by laws that exist within the theory that connect the change with other events already accounted for by the theory. One does not need to go outside the theory to find the basis for explaining the change. The situation is very different in the mental scheme. Here theories are not self-sufficient. A change in one's mental scheme requires the entire pattern of interlocking and connecting beliefs to be considered and possibily revised. In accommodating a change in a mental theory one must adjust an entire belief structure to account for such a change because the meaning of a mental event stems from its place in a coherent pattern of beliefs, desires and intentions. Mental events are governed by the ideal of rationality. When faced with an event to be accounted for we try to place it in a context which coheres with the event even if this requires us to revise our understandings of other mental events which we are willing to attribute to the person. In a word, in order to make sense of a mental event we try to make it make sense.

In summary, mental and physical predicates have different commitments. With mental events there is the commitment to the ideal of rationality; with physical predicates there is no commitment to make the event appear to be rational. The difference, then, between mental and physical predicates stems from our belief in humans as rational animals. Because of these disparate commitments, the two kinds of predicates serve different purposes and so statements relating the physical to the mental, and those relating the mental to the physical, are not lawlike. From this we can conclude that although there may be true statements relating the mental to the physical, these statements are not laws.

A second general feature of social sciences is that they provide lawful connections between events. An established scientific claim is not one that simply reports the co-existence of events; it tells us that one event occurs because another one occurs. The events are related in a lawlike manner such that if one event occurs the other is expected to occur.[11] This is, of course, a feature that is required in science for this is, in part, what it means for something to be a scientific law. If this feature did not hold in the social sciences there would be no reason to identify these fields as sciences at all. This also provides the basis for understanding what a necessary connection in the social sciences is. Because scientific laws tell us that events are related in a lawlike way we know that the connection between the events is not accidental; rather, the relation is such that if one occurs the other must occur. The second event is a necessary outcome of the first. Science, then, tells us that the second event is, in a sense, inevitable given the occurrence of the first. If the first could occur without the second we could not attribute a lawlike relation between the events.

This characteristic of social science raises interesting questions about, in particular, educational theory. If educational theory consists of social sciences alone, which is the view under consideration, and if the point of educational theory is to inform practice by giving practitioners the power of agency over practice and not just understanding of the practice, then educational theory will consist of those laws from psychology and sociology that give necessary connections between events. It tells us what happens naturally and inevitably when a particular cause or state of affairs is the case. This imposes limitations on what an educational theory can deal with. Education is a social process which is instituted to bring about changes in people. There would be no point to education if it were concerned with what happened naturally. If a person's intelligence develops according to fixed laws, and there is nothing that can be done to change or affect this development, then the development of a person's intelligence is not a matter for education. If there is nothing a teacher can do to change or affect how a person develops intellectually there is no point in the teacher trying to do something about it. It is only those things that the teacher can do something about that are the sorts of things that deserve the teacher's attention and consideration. Those elements of psychology and sociology that give such laws then are not candidates for inclusion in an educational theory of this sort. Developmental psychology is one area then, on this account, that would not seem to have a place in educational theory. Learning about invariant and universal stages of intellectual growth does not provide any information about how to educate people. While it may tell us what people at various stages of development are capable of doing, it does not become part of an educational theory because there is nothing that can be done by anyone about this development. Sociological laws of social class and stratification, as well, are irrelevant to educational theory if there is nothing that can be done by the teacher to alter or affect such arrangements.

Where psychology and sociology do have a place to play in educational theory is in providing laws that give the effects of actions that teachers and others involved in education can perform. If there is a law that relates a teacher action to a particular outcome such a claim becomes a candidate for inclusion in an educational theory. The laws of learning would seem to fit the bill. They seem to meet the requirement that the scientific laws of educational theory should enable those in education to be able to utilize them. Hilgard identified a number of experimental relationships on which learning theorists would agree regardless of their theoretical orientation. One is: "A motivated learner acquires what he learns more readily than one who is not motivated."[12] If this is true, and who would suggest that it is not, this statement could serve in an educational theory because it is both lawlike and under the control of the educator. A teacher can make learning occur more readily by providing learners with the motivation that will enable the ready acquisition of learning. Unlike the claims of, say, developmental psychology, this sort of claim is one that allows for intervention by agents and so can be the basis for educational actions.

Scientific theory and practice

I now want to consider how an educational theory conceived in this way informs practice. Nothing that has been said about this conception of educational theory shows it to be an inconsistent or illogical notion. A number of limitations have been identified but these do not show that this view of educational theory is one that should or ought to be rejected on purely philosophical grounds, at least at this point in the argument. The next test to put to this view is whether educational theory conceived as science can serve to guide and direct practice. Education is a clear example of a practical activity, by which I mean one in which human agents have goals or purposes which are to be brought about by actions they perform. In education the goals typically relate to learning, or more specifically to types of learning that are judged to be desirable by the agent or by the institution in which the agent participates. Not everything that can be learned is automatically included in an education program. Rather, decisions about what is to be learned stem from other values and purposes that give criteria for what is to be included. These criteria are influenced by the conception that we have of an educated person. Such a conception may or may not be widely held. Schools established and maintained by society will strive to realize a conception that meets widespread approval and reflects the basic values of that society. Depending on the society, it may include individual members of the society in the formulation of the basic values to be transmitted in the schools and in the administration of those values. In other societies, where the basic values are more rigid and less open to interpretation, the society may not allow participation in the setting of the goals of education; they may be imposed in a much more authoritarian or hierarchical manner. In a society in transition, for example, where the established authorities and institutions are attempting to reform or change the values of the society, the schools may be required to bring about learning that reflects a different conception of what the educated person is, often against the wishes of a substantial segment of the population. This is why the schools become such an important institution in revolutionary societies.[13] Other societies may be more tolerant of differing conceptions of the educated person. They may allow groups that hold views of what constitutes an educated person that are different from the dominant view of the society to establish their own schools where more localized conceptions can be realized. And finally, just to complicate matters, some societies may tolerate only a range of different conceptions in which case they will allow schools to pursue different conceptions of the ideal of education but will maintain some control over them to insure that the ideals pursued do not differ too radically from the standard ideal of education for that society.

An important goal of educational institutions is to bring about learning that reflects the ideal that is held for an educated person. But the learning that takes place is not just academic or intellectual learning. The ideal of an educated person includes, typically, social, personal and vocational learning as well as academic learning. A society will want its young to acquire certain knowledge about the world as reflected in academic disciplines, but it will also want its young to learn particular attitudes, values, tastes and standards of conduct that will in part determine the kind of people the young become. The schools are also entrusted with the responsibility of influencing the social development of the young so that they grow up to have certain attitudes towards their society and commitments towards the preservation and value of their culture. Finally, and this is a more recent responsibility placed on educational institutions, the schools have an economic function. They are to help insure that the young contribute to the economic life of their society, or, at least, that they do not become a drain on the economic system. How these goals are realized in a particular educational system is a complex matter. Indeed, the different values probably cannot be achieved independently. Learning particular personal attributes and learning particular academic disciplines may bring about vocational goals.

We need now to ask how our knowledge of education can influence how educational institutions go about realizing their goals. Educational theory, as I am now conceiving it, is essentially applied psychology and sociology. As has already been claimed educational theory is not a value or normative theory. It provides no way to make the judgments of value that are required in conceiving of the ideal that ought to be pursued in educational activities. It can, at best, describe the values that are in fact held in a society. Through the social sciences, and sociology in particular, we can learn what the values in a given society are and how the society's educational institutions manifest and promote those values. Social science can explain why certain learnings are included in the schools; it cannot justify those learnings. But, I would want to claim, the justification of what is done in education is an important, even fundamental, matter.

I want to establish this claim by showing that an educational practitioner cannot act simply on the basis of received values that are not to be questioned; the educator, that is, cannot avoid justification questions. Let us assume for the moment that a descriptive theory of values, such as that provided by sociology, is sufficient for guiding educational practice. This means that the educator can make all the educational decisions needed simply by knowing the values that are in fact established in one's society. There are two problems with this. First, the values that a society has for what counts as an educated person are not unitary or univocal. Our conception of what ought to happen in schools does not determine what it is that educators should do. Vocational goals may dictate the development of particular, occupation related, skills, while academic goals may require the teaching of highly general skills. A society may value a high degree of independence or autonomy as a personal value, but require cooperation and submission to the views of the majority as a social value. The possibility of internal conflict within the ideals of the society means that educators cannot base their decisions on a simple knowledge of what is valued in society. The second problem is the distance between the educational values of a society which can be known through sociology and the actual context in which the educator works. Knowing that the cultural traditions of a society should be passed on to the young (a typical educational value in a society) does not determine what particular subjects or topics should be taught in the schools or how they should be taught. So, the assumption that a descriptive knowledge of the ideal of the educated person is sufficient for educational practice does not hold. The educator, in order to make the appropriate decisions, must enter into discussions of value and to provide justifications for decisions. But this is precisely what is not included in educational theory.

Although an educational theory does not provide the basis for making normative judgments and even though educational practitioners cannot avoid making such judgments, educational theory may still have relevance to the practice of education. So far the situation is not unlike medical practice where the practitioner has to make normative judgments and where the theory does not include the grounds for making these judgments, but where science still provides guidance for practice. In order to pursue the issue of how theory can influence practice, I want to consider three possible ways in which it might be claimed that a theory has bearing upon practice. It seems to me that three possible ways of stating such a relation are to say that the theory tells what ought or ought not to be done in practice, that the theory tells what can be done in practice, and that the theory tells what cannot be done in practice.

The discussion so far nearly answers the question of whether a theory can tell us what ought or ought not be done in practice; the answer is in the negative. Since a scientific theory quite explicitly does not contain a normative element and has no way of establishing value claims as being justified, it cannot tell us what we ought or ought not to do. As we have seen, the educational practitioner must make judgments about what ought and ought not to be done. These questions cannot be relegated to some other forum. That is, in the ordinary practice of education, teachers and educators cannot avoid making these decisions; they are not decisions which can be left to others and provided to practitioners as givens. All practitioners must answer normative questions for themselves. The relation between theory and practice would have to be construed as an argument in which theoretical premises imply or support practical conclusions. If the practical conclusion is a normative claim, as is the case in the view under consideration, then the theoretical premises must contain at least one premise that is itself normative. This is clearly true if the relation between the premises and the conclusion is the implication relation. It is a commonplace of logic that non-normative premises cannot imply normative conclusions.

It is less clear in the case of the supporting relation. That is, if we view the relation between theoretical claims and practical claims as one in which theoretical premises provide support for, but do not imply, practical conclusions, then it is not clear that scientific premises cannot provide support for normative conclusions. In order to examine this question consider the following case, adapted from an essay by Brophy,[14] in which scientific statements support, but do not imply, a normative practical claim. Research on classroom management has shown that it is not possible to distinguish good teachers from poor teachers on the basis of how they respond to discipline problems or to the infraction of rules in the classroom. The difference between such teachers is seen, rather, in the techniques they use for preventing such problems from arising in the first place. Good teachers are those who see classroom management "more as a matter of instruction, telling and showing students what you want them to do, than as forcing them to do something that they already know how to do."[15] One of the characteristics of teachers who have the ability to prevent such problems and consequently "to set up and maintain the classroom as an effective learning environment,"[16] has been labelled "withitness" or the ability of teachers to "monitor what is going on around the classroom, and [to] show the students that he or she is 'with it,' (aware, likely to spot what is going on early, likely to know who has started something if somebody starts something)."[17] So, "withitness" is a feature of effective classroom management, which leads to the establishment of an effective learning environment, so we can conclude that teachers ought to be prepared to be "with it."

Here we have what appears to be a normative practical statement which is the conclusion of an argument which contains no normative premises. The premises are either definitions, as of the definition of "withitness", or research findings. The premises do not imply the conclusion, but do support it. But, it turns out, the support the premises give for the conclusion comes from an unstated assumption. This argument has no force if one does not admit the desirability of maintaining an effective learning environment. If one is not committed to this value or norm, then there is no point in accepting the claim that one ought to do something to promote the assumed value. So, even if we relax the relation between scientific claims and practical claims from "implies" to "supports," we find that the relation does not hold on its own; we must add a value assumption to the scientific claims in order to get support for the practical claim. In conclusion then, a scientific theory of education does not tell us what we ought to do or what we ought not to do in practice.

The next question to consider is whether a scientific theory of education can tell us what we can do in practice. Using the above example the conclusion for practice in this case would be that the learning environment can be enhanced if the teacher is "with it." This statement is logically implied by the theoretical statements as given so the problem identified in the earlier case does not arise here. There is a different kind of problem here that blocks the move from the scientific theory to the realm of practice. In this case the problem is that the conditions under which the theoretical statements are true are different from those in which the practical statement is true. A theoretical statement is necessarily abstracted from experience. It is not about a particular case; rather it is about cases of a particular kind which are described by the conditions under which the statement holds. A scientific claim, or research finding, gives a relation that holds generally. It needs to specify conditions under which the relation holds. But not every possible condition is included in a scientific law; if a law attempted to do this it would have no generality. So part of a scientific claim is that many possible conditions are held to be irrelevant to the application of a research finding. In education, for example, research will look for results that may be dependent on such characteristics or conditions as the learner's sex, social condition, ethnic background or learning ability. Educational research rarely, if ever, considers conditions such as the learner's eye color, spats at the breakfast table, friendship networks, or previous personal experience with the topic being learned. All of these conditions may potentially influence a child's learning or affect the learning environment. The scientific claim, though, cannot take into account all such conditions. The researcher must select some variables, usually on the basis of the psychological or sociological theory brought to the research situation, to focus on in the research and to ignore or treat as irrelevant all other conditions that may occur. In educational research, as in other social scientific contexts, the technique of randomization is used to make other conditions irrelevant. The results, then, of scientific research apply generally across the identified variables.

In the practical context, however, the situation is different. Here, the practitioner will take into account more conditions than are typically allowed for in the scientific claim. In the first place the practitioner has access to more information about the learners and the context of their learning than can be included in the research claim. The particular characteristics and quirks of the learners can be incorporated into the practitioner's reasoning about what should be done in a specific situation. As well, the practitioner has information about the context in which the learning takes place. Previous learning, social conditions, even the weather, provide the practitioner with information that may be relevant to what children can learn at a particular juncture, but these are the sorts of things that get excluded from consideration in research. The block between theory and practice in this case is that the information the practitioner has may be sufficient to override the scientific finding in a particular case. Take again the example of "withitness." The claim here is that in general teachers who are "with it," and so can anticipate problems in the classroom and who appear to know what is going on in the classroom at all times, can enhance the learning environment in the classroom. One of the conditions of teaching that is ignored in this sort of research is the physical presence of the teacher, what the teacher looks like. It seems plausible to say that a teacher with a forceful, strong, even intimidating, appearance may be able to prevent classroom management problems without having to be "with it." That is, the teacher, simply through a threatening demeanor, may be able to prevent problems without being able to monitor what is going on in the classroom. Alternatively, a teacher, through some events, may have lost all credibility with students so that no matter how "with it" he is, the class will not respond. Thus, it may be the case that a research finding may be true, but in particular cases it may not be true because conditions which have been judged to be irrelevant in the research context have become central in the practical context. This shows that there is a block between what is known through research and what can be done in practice.

This discussion points to an important difference between the theoretical and practical realms. Different interests matter in the different areas. In research one's interest is to find what holds generally or even universally. This means that one decides before the case that many possible conditions are irrelevant in order to achieve generality. In the practical realm, one is dealing with a specific set of conditions, and one typically wants to know how to handle that particular situation. Here, the variables judged to be irrelevant in the theoretical context may well become important issues. Because in the one case specific features must be ignored and in the other specific features cannot be ignored, theory often does not tell what can be done in practice.

If a scientific theory of education cannot tell us what ought or ought not to be done or what can be done in practice, perhaps it will tell us what cannot be done in practice. The role an educational theory may have in practice is to set limits on what can be done in the practical realm. Instead of giving advice or direction as to what to do, the theory may provide the boundary conditions for practice. This is surely a possible view of the role of theory. Scientific laws, as I have already claimed, present what is in a sense inevitable. They give us necessary connections between events such that if the cause or antecedent event occurs the consequent or subsequent event must occur inevitably. In a sense then, science tells us about those kinds of happenings that once they start we are powerless to control. This gives us information about the practical realm because there we want to stay within what it is that practitioners have control over. So such knowledge can be helpful.

A scientific theory can be seen to set negative limits, or what cannot be done, on practice in the following way. A plausible interpretation of the work of Jean Piaget is to claim that he has formulated laws of intellectual development which describe the way in which any person necessarily and inevitably acquires concepts and strategies for interpreting and understanding the world.[18] If what Piaget claims is true, then the educational practitioner cannot do anything to circumvent these laws of development. That is, if children at age five cannot use formal operations, the teacher is ill-advised to include materials for children at this age that require formal operations. While the theory does not tell us what can or ought to be done, it does tell us the sorts of things that cannot be done and so in this way provides some guidance for practice.

The question now is whether this view can be maintained or whether in spite of its initial plausibility it, too, is a problematic position. First it should be noted that if it is a sustainable position, it is a quite minimal account of the relation of theory and practice. A theory that gives the practitioner advice on what cannot be done in a particular circumstance leaves open the question of what can or should be done. Knowing, say, that young children cannot handle abstract reasoning (according to Piaget) tells the practitioner nothing about what to do with those children in order to educate them.

I now want to offer some considerations to suggest that a scientific educational theory is not sufficient to set limits on practice. My first point is similar to that offered to show that such a theory is not sufficient to give guidance on what can be done in practice. A scientific claim is general in that it specifies that under certain conditions a particular event or state must occur. Any conditions not stated in the scientific claim are held to be irrelevant to the application of the general statement. But in the practical realm certain conditions may obtain that are crucial but which in general are irrelevant. For example, while it may be the case that in general children at the age of five are not capable of dealing with abstract reasoning, an educational practitioner may be faced with a child with a particular and unusual background who is able to deal quite effectively with abstract thought. Such a case is not to be taken as a counter-example to the original claim. The statement that under conditions $C_1, C_2, \ldots C_n$, E will normally occur is not shown to be false by the existence of the particular case that under condition C_r, E does not occur. Social scientific claims are given in a form of probability, that in general something probably occurs. So cases such as this do not disprove the original claim.

Again, this point shows the different interests at stake in the theoretical and practical realms. When one is working at the theoretical level one is concerned to determine what happens as a matter of course or what is generally true. One is deliberately not concerned with the details of particular cases. At the practical level one is faced with a particular problem or issue that needs resolution or solution. What is true in general is not at issue. Rather one is concerned with particular details and the proposed solution does not have to have any applicability to other circumstances. So, the limits set by an educational theory that hold in general may not be actual limits in a particular case.

A second consideration for the insufficiency of scientific educational theory for setting limits on what can be done in practice stems from the fact that the social sciences, which are drawn upon in an educational theory, deal with human action.[19] An educational theory will produce laws that describe regularities in human action. The social sciences, by definition, are concerned with what human beings do, and to produce lawlike claims about humans it must determine and describe what it is about humans that happens regularly and necessarily. Human action, though, is malleable in ways that natural phenomena are not. The laws of the natural sciences give regularities of events that cannot be changed by the objects described. That the pressure of a gas varies with temperature and inversely with volume is something that cannot be changed by gasses. That seals in the Arctic construct and maintain breathing holes in the ice is not something that can be changed by seals. That humans cannot digest cellulose is not something we can alter. However, in the social sciences many of the regularities that are found are themselves learned in social contexts and possibly can be changed. Patterns of authority in a culture can be, and have been, changed when that culture comes into contact with another. Regularities that hold in a society under a particular economic system can be changed if the society changes its economic order. Observed regularities of learning may be a function of how a society goes about teaching its young, and if the teaching should change different regularities of learning may result. This is particularly true in the educational context. Here it is quite clear that the regularities that one might find about education and schools are the result of instituted social practices for the teaching of the young. If different practices are developed quite different regularities might result. Thus, the claims of educational theory need not set limits for practice. The regularities themselves are the result of practical decisions and if other decisions are made the regularities might or will change.

Given this discussion, an educational theory is not sufficient for setting limits on practice because the theory itself is in part a result of past and current practice. The theory would set limits if it were the case that practice could not be altered. Educational practice is just the sort of thing that can and does change, and because it does change observed regularities may change. So we have no grounds to conclude that if we have an educational theory, it gives us guidance about what cannot be done in practice.

To summarize, when we conceive of educational theory as a scientific theory there is no direct relation of a conceptual sort between the theory and actual practice.[20] An educational theory does not tell us, by itself, what we should do, what we should not do, what we can do, or what we cannot do. In other words, an educational theory is not sufficient for directing practice. This is not to say that there is not a role for scientific educational theory. It may provide us with an understanding of what happens in education and with a basis for explaining educational phenomena and events. The force of my remarks is that there is no basis for the belief that if we provide a person with a scientific educational theory we have at the same time provided the person with grounds for guiding one's educational practice.

Applications of the scientific view

In spite of the criticisms of the view of educational theory as being scientific, it is the dominant view, particularly in the educational research community. Here the standards, practices and commitments of the social sciences are most evident. Although most would agree that educational research has not provided an educational theory that meets the expectations that have been adumbrated above for a scientific theory, the ideal towards which we should be striving is a theory that meets all the expectations of a well-formed theory in the social sciences. I now want to examine two accounts of science in education in the light of the discussion and criticisms I have provided for such a view. In doing so I hope to give additional support and clarification for the position I have developed.

The scientific base for the art of teaching

N. L. Gage in *The Scientific Base for the Art of Teaching*[21] spends some time discussing the role of science in understanding teaching.

Although this is not the focus of his work, he is more concerned to develop a scientific base for teaching and teacher education, what he says about science is suggestive of the view I have offered. I want to show, however, that the view I have presented goes more deeply than his.

Gage begins his discussion of this topic by distinguishing between the art of teaching and the science of teaching. Teaching is a "practical art" which is to say that it is a "process that calls for intuition, creativity, improvisation and expressiveness."[22] If teaching is seen in this way it becomes possible to understand it according to criteria that are used in discussing other arts. That is, teaching can be discussed as a critic or connoisseur would discuss any work of art. But this is not the direction Gage wants to pursue. He wants to develop the scientific basis on which the art of teaching rests. He sees an understanding of teaching as coming from both its nature as a practical art and its having a scientific base. This suggests that he would claim that the scientific base alone is not sufficient for understanding teaching; we need as well to see it as a practical art. Indeed he makes claims that come very close to this sort of language. When he says, "If the behavioral scientist has no monopoly of serious concern with teaching, neither has the aesthetician,"[23] he is suggesting that neither approach is sufficient for providing a theory of teaching.

He next distinguishes between a scientific theory of teaching and a scientific base for the art of teaching. A science of teaching, "implies that good teaching will some day be attainable by closely following rigorous laws that yield high predictability and control."[24] This view is alleged to be erroneous because it would eliminate the elements of creativity, intuition and judgment that are part of the practical art of teaching. He argues the point by using the analogy with medicine and engineering. "In medicine and engineering, where the artistic elements are unquestionable, a scientific base can also be developed."[25] Although one may want to question whether the analogy holds, for Gage it is obvious. "The physician works with a thousand variables that have been identified and related to other variables by scientific methods. . . . But the physician uses the variables in what must be considered an artistic way as he approaches each new patient."[26] A scientific base for the art of teaching, which is something we can strive for, will use scientific methods for determining the relationships between and among variables. These relationships can, then, be used by teachers in creative, intuitive (i.e. artistic) ways. The scientific basis for the art of teaching will "consist of knowledge of regular, nonchance relationships in the realm of events with which the practice is concerned."[27]

To this extent Gage's position is consistent with what I have said. Social science can give us knowledge about the relationships in teaching, and presumably in education generally, but that knowledge is not sufficient for guiding practice. For Gage, the artistic elements of teaching seem to go beyond the scientific knowledge we have of teaching, but they are also necessary for the practice of teaching. However, as Gage begins to discuss the kinds of knowledge that scientific methods can provide a somewhat different picture begins to emerge. Consider this claim:

> Scientific method can contribute relationships between variables taken two at a time and even, in the form of interactions, three or perhaps four or more at a time. Beyond say four, the usefulness of what science can give the teacher begins to weaken, because teachers cannot apply, at least not without help and not on the run, the more complex interactions. At this point, the teacher as artist must step in and make clinical, or artistic, judgments about the best ways to teach. In short, the scientific base for the art of teaching will consist of two-variable relationships and lower-order interactions. The higher-order interactions between four and more variables must be handled by the teacher as artist.[28]

There is no reason in principle why scientific methods must be restricted to relationships involving four or fewer variables. Any number of variables can be inserted into scientific studies. What keeps the number down is our inability to cope with the complexity of such relationships and, perhaps, our inability to think up large numbers of relevant variables. Gage's point, then, is that the artistic element is needed in teaching because of our inability to deal with complex scientific relationships, not because science itself is inadequate to provide the relationships. It is perfectly consistent with Gage to claim that if humans were able to deal with such complex relationships we could dispense with the artistic element of teaching. The science of teaching is not possible only because of human frailty; there is nothing about science itself that prevents it from giving a complete account of teaching.

This is quite different from the account I presented. My claim is that a scientific theory of education is not sufficient for guiding educational practice no matter how many variables human beings are able to cope with. For Gage, a science of teaching is not possible only because of the relative inability of humans to cope with complexity.

So, in Gage we see a fundamental commitment to the conceptualization of educational theory as scientific. This is revealed, I think, in the following passage.

> Since *Summerhill* appeared in 1960, we seem to have more than ever been at the mercy of powerful and passionate writers who shift educational thinking ever more erratically with their manifestoes. The kind of research I have been describing is a plodding enterprise, the reports of which are seldom, I regret to say, as well written as the pronouncements of authors unburdened by scientific method. But, in the long run, the improvement of teaching—which

is tantamount to the improvement of our children's lives—will come in large part from the continued search for a scientific basis for the art of teaching.[29]

Perhaps, one example from Gage's work will show how he employs the kind of distinctions he makes. He and his co-workers reviewed the research on teacher behavior and classroom activity to develop statements "as to how third-grade teachers should work if they wish to maximize achievement in reading and, we think, also in mathematics, for children either higher or lower in academic orientation."[30] These statements are intended to be "relatively specific, objectively observable and require relatively little extrapolation from terminology to what is to be done."[31] One of these statements is, "When pupils work independently, teachers should insure that the assignments are interesting and worthwhile yet still easy enough to be completed by each third grader working without teacher direction."[32]

As advice to the teacher this is unexceptionable. The contrary recommendation would be to provide work for the students that is uninteresting, non-worthwhile or too difficult; but our reasons for rejecting this contrary advice have nothing to do with research, they have to do with the values and goals we bring to the teaching situation. That the work should be easy enough for the students to complete without teacher direction is, in this case, also not a matter of research, it follows from the specification of the work as independent work. Once we decide that the work should be done independently we are committed to finding work that the students can do without teacher direction; otherwise we would not be assigning independent work. So, although the statement may have been derived from research, as it stands its truth in no way depends upon that research.

But, although it is unexceptionable advice, it is extremely difficult advice to follow. To find material that is interesting, worthwhile, and easy enough to complete for twenty-five to thirty students in the third grade is no easy task. I find it difficult to find things for myself to do that meet these requirements. But to meet these requirements when one has to take into account the abilities, prior learnings and histories of others is surely a challenge. The original claim, the scientific base for teaching, then provides little information about the practice of teaching; it in fact tells us something for which we do not need to do research to establish its truth. In this case all the difficult and interesting questions are in the realm of what Gage allows to be, somewhat reluctantly, the judgmental or artistic realm of teaching.

The application of teacher effectiveness research

In an article relating some of the work in the research on teacher effectiveness to teacher education, Brophy states a position similar to the one just considered.

For the first time there is available a developing scientific data base, admittedly small and in other ways criticizable, but also very real, about linkages between teacher behavior and student outcomes. It is important for teacher educators to recognize that and begin to deal with it, not in some over-simplified or routinized way, but by beginning to make distinctions in their heads and in their students' heads between what is simply opinion and what is fact, and to try to include as many facts as possible in the teacher education program. At the same time, however, they need to be clear in their heads (and make clear in their students') that the facts do not prescribe courses of action but merely inform about the available options among which teachers have to choose.[33]

Now, what are some of these facts that have been found that relate teacher behavior and classroom activity? One relates to instructional time: "Teachers who allocate more time to academic instruction, other things being equal, have their students learn more academic content."[34]

Again, at first glance this seems to be an uninformative claim. It says that the more time a teacher spends teaching, the more the students will learn. But who would have thought otherwise? The claim is expanded in the following way: "The time that keeps coming up as important to students' learning is not just any time. It is time where students are actively attentive and engaged in purposeful activities for one thing, not time spent in busy work or something like that. Most importantly, it is time spent being actively instructed by or at least under the immediate supervision of the teacher."[35]

Even in the expanded form, the claim provides no direction for the practice of education. In order to make sense of the claim, it must be taken that there is a common presupposition as to what counts as purposeful work and what counts as busy work. The research findings hold only for purposeful work, but the research does not tell us how to separate such work from non-purposeful work. This must be done by the teacher who brings to the teaching situation an understanding of what the point of the teaching is and the ability to make judgments as to the experiences of the students so that one can determine what is meaningful for them. Again the research base provides minimal knowledge for the practice of teaching.

Brophy ends his article with an analogy to show the importance of developing a scientific base for teaching. Since the analogy is with medicine, which was a starting point for this chapter, I would like to consider it.

Think about Hippocrates, recognizably among the greatest physicians of all time. Suppose that you are suddenly doubled up with acute pain and you need help in a hurry. Somehow or other Hippocrates has come to life and opened up an office next to your local clinic or hospital. Would you go see Hippocrates or would you go to your local clinic or hospital? Anyone in his or her right mind would go to the local clinic or hospital. Why? Because as brilliant as

Hippocrates was, he had very little solid, useful knowledge about medicine compared to what is available today. Furthermore, when one visits a medical doctor, one expects competence. One wants treatment based on the latest, best established knowledge and skill pertaining to the diagnosis of the problem. One would not expect the doctor to intimate that the diagnosis and prescription of the treatment will be made according to some idiosyncratic philosophy; somebody like that is labelled a quack or a schizophrenic.[36]

Suppose, however, that in your local high school, where it happens that you have some choice over who your children's teachers will be, the two social studies teachers are Mr. Smith, a recent graduate of one of the best teacher education programs in the land, and Socrates. A parent who chooses Socrates as his or her child's teacher would not automatically be judged to be out of his or her right mind. While in medicine possession of the latest and best knowledge may well be sufficient for choosing a physician, this does not seem to be the basis for choosing one's teacher. The qualities that go into making a good teacher are not simply the knowledge of the latest research findings in education, which are doubtless important, or even the ability to employ those findings. Something more is required that is not captured by a science of education. It is in this way that the analogy with medicine breaks down.

CHAPTER 3

An epistemology of practice

A different perspective on the relation of theory and practice is given by Donald A. Schön in *The Reflective Practitioner*[1]. Schön's concern is that the traditional epistemology of professional practice, that of applied science, is unable to account adequately for the work of a professional practitioner. On the other hand, he does not want to align himself with radical critiques of professions which accord them no special knowledge. To avoid these two sorts of mistakes he develops an epistemology of reflective practice, provides examples of how it can be displayed in a variety of professions and discusses the general implications for the professions if reflective practice were to be the norm. I want to present his epistemology of reflective practice, make some criticisms of it and discuss how it might be useful in clarifying the relation of theory and practice in teaching and teacher education.

The critique of technical rationality

His account of reflective practice is presented in opposition to the notion of technical rationality which he describes as the dominant view in the education and preparation of professionals. Technical rationality says that once there is agreement on the ends, the question of how one ought to act can be reduced to instrumental questions of what means are best suited to the achievement of the end. If it is agreed to build a bridge across a river from point A to point B, it is the task of the engineer to design, using her professional skills and techniques, the best means of constructing the bridge. As this example suggests, and is held to be true in technical rationality in general, problems are solved by the application of scientific theory and techniques. The professional's task, when faced with a problem, is to draw upon the scientific base of the field to devise a solution. Technical rationality is characterized by presenting knowledge as being "specialized, firmly bounded, scientific and standardized."[2] It is specialized in that the knowledge used by a professional cannot be used by one in a different field. It is firmly bounded in that the boundaries between professional fields are clear. It is scientific in that, as already mentioned, professional knowledge is derived from basic scientific knowledge. Finally, it is standardized in that once solutions are found for problems they become standard solutions for similar problems.

Schön identifies three problems with the model of technical rationality that make it unsuitable as a general epistemology of practice. First, a survey of the work of professionals shows that often the problems they face are complex, uncertain, unstable, unique or present value conflicts. Technical rationality requires that knowledge be specialized, firmly bounded, scientific and standardized; these are just the characteristics that often fail to be present in practice. The problem of building a bridge from A to B that our engineer faced is not as simple as it appeared. In such a case there are environmental, political and aesthetic considerations, at least, that must be attended to as well as the design and structural considerations. As well, in this case the range of considerations makes the problem unique in that the same set of variables is unlikely to repeat itself. In a case where political and aesthetic concerns are present, such as in the building of a bridge, there may well be a shifting of positions and change in opinions. This would help to make the problem uncertain and unstable. Finally, the presence of political and aesthetic considerations introduces the possibility that there will be a conflict of values in this situation. It seems clear that what is not present in this situation as now described is a solution to the problem of building a bridge that is specialized, firmly bounded, scientific and standardized. So, Schön's first criticism of the technical rationality model is that it is not applicable to many of the problems faced by professional practitioners.

The second problem that the model of technical rationality faces is that it ignores the issue of problem setting. In this model the problem itself is given; the model is only concerned with the issue of solving the problem. However, in the work of the professional, the first task that needs to be done is to determine the problem to be solved. Often this is the most difficult and recalcitrant part of the practitioner's work. In medicine, which has as strong a scientific basis as any of the professions, the task of diagnosis is often identified as that part of the field which is not covered by the model of technical rationality. The diagnostician is often unable to verbalize the procedures which are used in making a diagnosis; there are few, if any, standardized techniques that can be invoked. The same point holds in all professions. To frame the problem that is to be solved requires attention to the specific case at hand which is viewed in the light of the professional experience of the practitioner. Such a task is not clearly one of applied science.

The final problem is that the model of technical rationality assumes that there is no value conflict and that there are no competing paradigms of practice. In this model the professional's task is to implement the solution to a problem; it is required that the value questions be settled prior to the entry of the professional into the situation. Also, the model requires that there are standardized procedures for providing the solution. However, these requirements are often not met. In the profession of town planning the practitioner is faced with a variety of values that can be in conflict, such as the need to revitalize a neighborhood, to provide a stock of affordable housing and to promote the economic growth of the city. These are values which have their supporters and which often cannot all be met. The town planner does not work in an environment in which the value questions have all been settled before the practitioner can begin to work. In the previous chapter I argued that in teaching as well the value issues cannot be settled prior to the teacher's interactions with students. Competition among paradigms of problem solving is exemplified by the field of psychiatry. There are competing models of how to go about doing psychiatry which are hotly debated within the field with respect to their desirability and effectiveness. The psychiatrist does not work in an environment where there are standardized techniques for solving problems.

Reflective practice

With these difficulties in the model of technical rationality Schön concludes that it fails to portray the nature of knowledge found in professional practice. He wants to develop an alternative epistemology, which he calls reflective practice, that will better account for practical knowledge and will rectify the problems that he has identified which exist between the practice of a profession and its relation to its clients, institutions and society.

As a first step in the development of his alternative epistemology, Schön discusses what he calls knowing-in-action, or what has been called by others knowing how or tacit knowledge. This is the knowledge inherent in intelligent action. When people possess knowledge of how to do something, they know how to carry out the action spontaneously. Driving a car is a clear example of an action that can be performed intelligently. A person who knows how to drive a car does not have to sit at the wheel and rehearse his knowledge of how to drive. Rather, he simply begins to drive; the motor is started, seat belts fastened, the car is put into gear and off he goes. One does not need to stop and think about what to do; it is done automatically. But to say that it is automatic is not to say that it is uninformed or unintelligent. How intelligently the person performs the action is displayed by the person's performance. We have no qualms about describing a person's driving as unintelligent if the person is continually causing accidents or havoc on the roads. So, even though the actions are performed spontaneously or automatically, they can be described as intelligent or foolish. They are not automatic in the way that, say, digestion is where it makes no sense to say that a person is digesting intelligently or foolishly. Another feature of knowing-in-action that Schön identifies is that the person is often unaware of having learned what he or she is able to do. Many component actions of driving a car, such as judging braking distance and deciding when it safe to enter a main road from a side street, are such that one learns them from experience but cannot say when it was learned. They develop over time, but acquiring them is important in helping to make the person an intelligent driver. A final feature of knowing-in-action is that people are usually unable to describe the knowing that their actions reveal. It would be very difficult, for example, to describe to someone how to know when to drive into a main street from a side street, except in unrevealing ways as: "Drive out when it is safe" or "Drive out when all the other cars are far enough away from the intersection." It is much simpler to show a person how to do it or to give the person corrective comments or instructions while that person performs the action. Starting from a basis of knowledge that is displayed in action rather than by statement, that one learns unawares, and that one usually cannot describe, gives Schön a very different starting point from that utilized by the model of technical rationality that would start from a basis of propositional knowledge.

A person's actions are not always spontaneous or automatic. When one's actions cause something that is surprising to the agent, he or she may have to stop and think about what to do. Schön calls this reflecting-in-action. While driving a car, the engine might start to make an unusual noise. Probably, the driver had been completely oblivious to the sound of the engine so long as it was normal. But as soon as it becomes unusual, the driver's attention is focused on the surprising sounds. The driver now will have to make a decision about what to do. While continuing to drive he or she will reflect upon the most desirable course of action, whether to pull off the road immediately, to head for the nearest service station or to ignore the sound as unimportant. The driver's experience and background knowledge will no doubt be important in determining what to do, but the person keeps driving the car through all these ruminations. To put this in Schön's language, while the person is reflecting-in-action about what to do the person is still knowing-in-action how to drive the car. It is this ability to reflect while one is performing an action that lies at the base of Schön's epistemology.

Schön next focuses on the knowledge and reflection exhibited by a professional practitioner which he calls knowing-in-practice and reflecting-in-practice. Reflecting-in-practice is occasioned when the phenomenon the practitioner faces eludes the ordinary categories of knowledge-in-practice. When physicians meet patients whose ailments do not fit any standard descriptions or when treatments do not act in predicted ways, they engage in reflection-in-practice. In such a case the practitioner constructs a theory of the unique case. By this Schön means that the practitioner attends to the particular case at hand as a singular instance, not as an exemplification of a type that might be dealt with through standard techniques. In attending to the unique case, the practitioner must first frame a problem. In doing so the practitioner defines the ends and the means interactively. After the problem has been set, the practitioner conducts experiments which either affirm or negate the proposed solution. If the solution is affirmed, the problem is regarded as being solved.

Before going on to consider the structure of reflective practice in more detail, an example may help to clarify this brief description. A teacher is faced with a child who is not learning. Under this description of the situation there is little if anything to suggest what might be done and so the teacher is stuck. In reflective action the teacher would attend to this unique situation and would attempt to reframe the problem. Utilizing experience the teacher might reframe the problem to one of physical impairment, say, hearing impairment. Under this reframed situation the teacher realizes that in order for the student to learn, he or she must be physically closer to the teacher so that the hearing difficulty would be minimized. Here the teacher is dealing with the end, enabling the student to learn, and the means, changing the child's physical locale in the classroom, interactively. The teacher then conducts a "thought experiment." The teacher realizes that the child's social difficulties on the playground and the child's slowness to respond to verbal instructions could also be due to a hearing impairment. In this way, the implications the teacher identifies affirm the reframed problem, and so the teacher takes the steps called for when one has a hearing impaired student.

Reflecting on reflective practice

I will now consider in turn the two central features of reflection-in-action: reframing the problem and on-the-spot experimentation. When practitioners are faced with an unexpected, nonroutine or surprising situation, in order to be reflective, they must reframe the situation to make it a problem that can be dealt with. A practitioner will approach the problem situation as a unique case, one that cannot be handled by applying standard theories or techniques. Because the standard ways are not helpful, the first step for the practitioner is to formulate the problem. In reframing a situation, the practitioner is trying to turn it into a tractable problem. The practitioner seeks to understand the situation and to redescribe it as one he can try to solve. Reframing a problem is an attempt to see the situation as something else, something with which the practitioner can deal. The practitioner brings a repertoire of examples, images, understandings and actions to the situation. From her experience she is able to see the situation in a new light. Our teacher saw the situation as a case of hearing impairment. A physician sees a blotch on the skin as a fungus infection. The practitioner does not go through a checklist in such a situation, she simply sees the situation in a new or different light. It is this ability to see a problem in a tractable way that constitutes the reframing of a problem. So the practitioner attends to a unique case which is intractable as it stands. By reframing it, she sees it in a way that she can deal with.

At this point it is not clear why Schön puts such emphasis on the problem being unique. There is a minimal sense in which it is clear that the problem is unique. The practitioner is dealing with a situation raised by a particular surprising situation. The teacher is dealing with a student, the physician with a patient, the architect with a site. Each has a single, or unique, problem which claims her attention. But this would seem to be the only way we can say the situation is unique. To make the situation tractable, the practitioner is to see it as something else. But to see something as something else is to see it under a description. The teacher sees the child under the description of being hearing impaired. The practitioner relies on her experience to provide the descriptive categories that can be used in particular cases. To put some case under a description is to see the case as an instance of a descriptive category which is a general class. Hence, it would seem that the situation is no longer taken to be unique but is now regarded as one instance of a general type. In Schön's process of problem setting, once the problem has been set by reframing it in terms of some other general descriptive category it would not seem to be unique any longer. That is, it has become another instance of a general category with which the practitioner is familiar. At this point there would seem to be nothing to preclude the practitioner from dealing with the situation according to the model of technical rationality. Once the situation has been formulated as an instance of a general type, the practitioner can use the standard theories and techniques for situations of this type. Schön seems not to have, at this point, given us grounds for abandoning technical rationality. Rather he has given us a basis for setting the problem, and he has rightly criticized technical rationality for being silent on this issue, but he has not given us grounds for not using technical rationality's mode of problem-solving. He has relied on the uniqueness of the situation as a ground for the inappropriateness of technical rationality. But as we have seen, his account requires only a trivial sense of uniqueness. His general point here is that the practitioner is to see the unique or particular situation as an instance of a type with which she is familiar. Once this is done there seems to be no reason why technical rationality is to be abandoned.

Schön explicitly disagrees with this interpretation; so I will consider his comment on this point and try to answer it. In his account of bringing past experience to bear upon a problematic situation he says,

> When a practitioner makes sense of a situation he perceives to be unique, he *sees* it *as* something already present in his repertoire. To see *this* as *that* is not to subsume the first under a familiar category or rule. It is, rather, to see the unfamiliar, unique situation as both similar to and different from the familiar one, without at first being able to say similar or different with respect to what.[3]

I want to consider his claim in two parts. The first is that using one's experience is not subsuming something under a category but is seeing something as similar to and different from something else in experience, and the second is that initially one cannot describe the similarities and differences. It is not clear that the distinction between subsuming something under a category and seeing something as similar to and different from something else in one's experience is a real distinction. When I see the object on my desk as a telephone, and note that in order even to begin the sentence I have to see it as something, namely an object, I am seeing it as being similar to and different from examples or images that are part of my repertoire of experience. It is similar to other telephones in that it allows me to talk to people at a great distance, it connects me to other telephones and it rings from time to time. It is different in color, shape and mechanisms from other telephones in my experience. So, I see it as something already in my repertoire. But seeing it as a telephone is to subsume the object under the category of telephones. Grammatically, what follows the words "seeing as" is a category word, not an individual word. When I see an animal as a dog, I use the category word "dog" and not individual names such as Spot or Rover.[4] To belong to a category is to share some features with other things that fall under the category and not to share some others. It is not the case, however, that the features will always be obvious or predictable. We can see things in ways that are novel, unusual or metaphorical, but this only says that we can subsume objects under categories in novel, unusual or metaphorical ways. Schön's example of the product developers who were trying to improve the design of a paintbrush beginning their successful work by seeing a paintbrush as a kind of pump[5] is both an example of seeing the paintbrush in a novel way and of subsuming it under a novel category. Schön's attempt to distinguish between seeing as and category subsumption is, then, unsuccessful. But is a difference restored by adding the proviso that initially one cannot describe the similarities and differences?

As the second part of his rejection of the identification of "seeing as" with "subsuming under a category," Schön says that in the case of seeing a problematic situation as an exemplar of something in one's repertoire, one at first cannot describe the differences and similarities between the new situation and the past experience. Schön would seem to be assuming that in the case of category subsumption one can describe at the outset the similarities and differences. Without such an assumption there would be no difference between category subsumption and seeing as on this point. But is it the case that one cannot subsume something under a category without being able at first to say in what respects it is similar to and different from other objects that fall under the same category? When I subsume the object on my desk under the category of telephones I do not tick off on some imaginary list its similarities to and differences from other telephones I have experienced in order to determine whether this is indeed a telephone; having the concept of telephone I simply look at it and see it as one. And, indeed, when I am asked why I have called it a telephone, I may not be able to describe similarities and differences without reflection; I might say that it just is a telephone. So, it seems that in the case of category subsumption one at first is not necessarily able to say in what respects the object is similar to and different from others in the same category.

So, I conclude that Schön's account of reframing a problematic situation in the light of the practitioner's experience does not warrant concluding that this activity is different from seeing the problem as an instance of a particular type. This is a serious point because it undermines a key linchpin in his effort to establish an epistemology of practice that is different from the model of technical rationality. This dominant model is based on the view that science can provide general answers to types of problems and that the practitioner needs only to apply those answers to particular instances of the problem. Schön has attempted to refute this claim by arguing that in practice the practitioner is dealing with a unique situation, not an instance of a general type. My argument has been that Schön's account is not sufficient to refute the claim of the model of traditional rationality.

The second central feature of Schön's epistemology of reflective practice is experimentation. In the model of traditional rationality, experimentation is both highly formalized and sharply separated from practice. It is highly formalized in that there is a clear logic of confirmation which sets bounds on what can be accepted and on how the experimenter can proceed. It is separated from practice in that the task of experimentation is largely relegated to researchers in educational institutions and not to practitioners. The practitioner is not to conduct experiments, rather such issues are turned over to researchers who then provide practitioners with answers that can be applied in practice. Schön's intention is to provide an account of experimentation and its logic that can be used by practitioners to integrate research and practice.

In professional practice, the norms of controlled experimentation can be met at best in only limited ways. The practitioner working in a particular situation with a particular problem is typically not in a position to control variables, nor is she in a position to stand back and view the situation from an objective, unbiased standpoint. The practitioner has an interest in the outcome of the experiment. As well, the practitioner is concerned with changing a particular situation whereas the researcher's interest is with understanding a class of phenomena and not primarily with changing particular instances. This prevents the practitioner from employing the logic of hypothesis testing in her work. In order to show how experimentation is used in reflective practice Schön identifies three kinds of experiment.[6]

The first kind of experiment is the exploratory experiment. This is the most general in that it probably captures the broadest sense of the word in ordinary language where one uses "experiment" to see what happens if something is done. A novice at the computer may experiment with it by touching a button to see what happens. A psychiatrist may make her office less austere and more homey to see what happens. A teacher may rearrange the seating in the classroom to see its effects. All of these are exploratory experiments. In each case the person had no hypothesis to test or specific change in mind when she performed the experiment. Rather, the person just wanted to see what would follow from a particular action.

The second kind of experiment is the move-testing experiment. Here the experimenter performs an action in order to produce an intended change. The computer novice wants to stop the running of a program and touches the key "Esc" to see if it will stop the program. The psychiatrist wants her patients to be more relaxed and so changes the decor of her office to see if this will result in such a change. The teacher wants to end the social isolation of certain children and so changes the seating arrangement to see what the effect will be. In each case the action may or may not bring about the intended change. If it does, the action is, according to Schön, affirmed; if not, it is negated.

The final kind of experiment is hypothesis testing. This is the kind of experimentation used in the model of technical rationality and in the sciences generally. When this kind of experiment is found in reflective practice, its logic is the same as when used in science. A hypothesis is formed that a change in one variable, the independent variable, will produce a change in another, the dependent variable. The remaining variables are controlled, and if the results of the test bear out the hypothesis, it is said to be confirmed; if not, it is said to be disconfirmed.

Schön maintains that, "when the practitioner reflects-in-action in a case he perceives as unique, paying attention to the phenomena and surfacing his intuitive understanding of them, his experimenting is at once exploratory, move-testing and hypothesis testing."[7] Although the logic of hypothesis testing is the same in reflective practice as in traditional rationality there are differences in the two contexts that stem from the practitioner's interest in change rather than understanding. First, the practitioner states the hypothesis in the imperative mood: "Let it be the case that X." In this way the practitioner makes the hypothesis true, the testing of the hypothesis "consists of moves that change the phenomena to make the hypothesis fit."[8] As well, some of the standards of controlled experimentation are not applied in practice. As the practitioner has an interest in the outcome of the experiment, because it is testing her hypothesis about a situation she is trying to change, she is not an objective, distant observer. The practitioner wants to confirm the hypothesis that she has formed. Because the situation can resist the practitioner's desire to have the hypothesis confirmed, Schön adds, these experiments are not completely self-fulfilling. In the case of reflective practice, the experimenter is part of the situation to be understood because the situation is partly of the experimenter's making. So, hypothesis testing is at the same time the test of a move and an exploratory probe.

There is also a difference between controlled experimentation and experimentation in reflective practice on the decision to stop the experiment. In controlled experimentation the researcher could in principle continue indefinitely because his concern is to refute competing hypotheses. As long as the experimenter can formulate hypotheses that might resist refutation greater than any so far tested, research can continue. In reflective practice, the concern is to change a situation; so, if a move brings about the intended consequences and any unintended outcomes are viewed as favorable, the purpose has been achieved and the experiment can conclude.

There are a number of puzzles raised by Schön's account of experimentation. Although the experiments of a reflective practitioner are claimed to be instances of all three kinds of experiment at the same time, the examples Schön gives are very different from those found in science.[9] The two cases he describes are both ones in which the practitioner is reviewing a situation with a student. In one a psychiatrist is working with a resident on how to handle a particular woman's problem. The practitioner's suggestion to the student is to treat the situation as a problem of transference, which is different from the way the student had seen it. In further discussion with the student, more details about the case lend support to the hypothesis that transference is the key. The practitioner here does not meet the patient and so can do nothing to test the hypothesis. What we have here can be called a "thought experiment." In science, and in traditional rationality, it would seem that the test of a hypothesis would require doing something, not just thinking about something. We would not say that the hypothesis that a particular drug cures cancer had been tested if the researcher had only conducted a thought experiment. Testing requires that an actual experiment be conducted. So, it is not clear what has happened to the original notion of a controlled experiment. It seems that Schön has extended the notion to include a much broader sort of activity so that what counts as the test of a hypothesis in reflective practice would not count as one in traditional rationality. As a result, the distinction between hypothesis testing and move testing seems to be lost. In that the practitioner's hypothesis is to change a situation and that she can test the hypothesis by only thinking about what would happen if the hypothesis were to be accepted, there is no difference between the practitioner's test of a hypothesis and her test of a move; they both come to the same thing. It was when hypothesis testing was governed by a strict logic of confirmation that there was a difference between it and move testing.

A second puzzle is whether we really have a difference between traditional rationality and reflective practice with respect to experimentation. Schön explicitly states that science engages in exploratory experiments and hypothesis testing experiments and, notwithstanding my comments above, that they are the same in each case. As well, it seems plausible to say that science engages in move-testing experiments. While it may not get included in the report of the experiment, which would only deal with the test of a hypothesis, the scientist will try things out to see if they bring about the intended consequences. An adjustment may be made to a piece of apparatus to see if it gives a better reading or a different animal may be used in a drug trial to see if a different result might obtain. So there seems to be room in science and traditional rationality for move-testing experiments. Hence, all three kinds of experiment are to be found in both traditional rationality and reflective practice. There are no grounds, then, to conclude that the account of experimentation in reflective practice is inconsistent with that in traditional rationality.

The upshot of this discussion is that Schön has not provided a distinctive epistemology of reflective practice. I have argued that the two central features of such an epistemology that Schön identifies, the setting of the problem and the conducting of an experiment, are not inconsistent with the epistemology of traditional rationality. So, he has not provided an account of reflective practice which distinguishes it conceptually from the model he is at pains to reject. I do not want, though, to conclude that Schön's account is to be rejected. The problems that he identifies with traditional rationality are real and the differences between reflective practice and the dominant mode are insightful. I now want to use what he says to provide a basis other than epistemology, which Schön tried, for the difference between traditional rationality and reflective practice.

The difference between traditional rationality and reflective practice can best be shown by following Schön's suggestions about the interests of the inquirer rather than by looking at the logic of the inquiry. This route is quite different; different interests do not imply different logics. To use the old example, one can study medicine both to learn to cure and to learn to kill. One can learn to teach in order to educate or to indoctrinate. Throughout his discussion, Schön makes many comments on how the practitioner's interests are different from that of the researcher. He is correct in pointing out that in the traditional model there is a sharp and hierarchical distinction between the researcher and the practitioner. In that model the practitioner faces different issues and problems than does the researcher. And it may well be a sound criticism of the dominant model to focus on this separation and to urge that inquiry be such that practitioners can engage in it. Let us now turn to some of these differences.

The first difference is that the researcher is concerned with the general and the practitioner with the particular. A practitioner, when faced with a problem, needs to find a solution to that problem; it is irrelevant to him whether the solution could be applied to other problems. The researcher, however, is working at a distance. She is not concerned with a particular instance; she is working with a class of instances. For her, a solution is not found until it worked for all, or a majority, of cases. Something that only worked in one case would not be a solution. A second difference is that the practitioner is typically interested in change and the researcher typically in understanding. It is clear that the practitioner facing a problem is seeking to change something, namely to solve the problem, and that his work will be done when the problem is solved. That the researcher is concerned with understanding and not change is not so clear. In basic science, it is clearly the case that the interest is understanding. That a finding in basic science would have no application and, hence, could change nothing, is not a problem in the least. In applied science, it is not so straightforward. Here the researcher may be motivated by the desire for both change and understanding. That understanding is the dominant interest is shown by the fact that if the researcher found a solution to one instance only, perhaps even the instance that occasioned her investigation, but this solution worked for no other case, the researcher's work would not be over. She would pursue the problem further in an attempt to understand the case better. In such a situation, however, the practitioner would take the solution and apply it, ignoring the other questions that still plague the researcher. Another important difference that Schön describes is that the practitioner is faced in the first instance with determining just what the problem is and that this is by no means an obvious or easy task. The researcher is faced with a different situation. For her, given the separation of research and practice, her problems are presented from practice. Her task is to generalize the problem and to design a research program to get at it. Further because of the separation of research and practice, a tradition of research may grow up which presents problems for research. When this occurs the problems do not come from practice. In educational psychology, for example, much of the research grows out of previous work in the discipline and may have no bearing at all on practice in schools.[10]

The difference between confirmation and affirmation that Schön describes is of particular importance. The researcher needs to show that her findings are confirmed according to strict canons of research. The practitioner needs only to show that a particular action affirms his hypothesis. The teacher who tries a new seating arrangement to solve a problem and finds that it works has affirmed a hypothesis. It seems beside the point to insist on the stronger requirement of confirmation, as defined in science, in such situations. Finally, the practitioner, unlike the researcher, is part of the situation. His intentions and actions are at work in the interpersonal context of the profession. Being an actor he cannot be an independent observer as is possible for the researcher.

Reflective practice in education

My concern now is to understand what can be made of the relation of theory to practice in education in the light of Schön's discussion of the reflective practitioner. Although he may not speak directly about the relation of theory to practice, he is certainly motivated by problems he identifies that exist in the dominant accounts of the professions concerning how research, or theory-based knowledge, is utilized by prac-titioners. As well, he can be read as proposing that theory be related to practice in ways different from that given in the dominant account. It is that reading I will try to explicate taking into account the criticisms I have made above.

The first task in reflective practice is the formulation of the problem. The well-prepared teacher will have a great deal of knowledge and ability at hand, but there will be times when this knowledge cannot be used in a spontaneous, nonreflective way. In such cases, where reflective practice is required, the teacher will have to formulate a problem which, we have seen, is to see the problematic situation under a different, and perhaps novel, description. The reflective teacher will have a repertoire of categories, examples, exemplars, images and the like to call upon in formulating problems. Since the first step in reflective practice is to see a situation under a different description, a person cannot be reflective without possessing a range of concepts under which particular cases can be described. The broader the range of concepts a person has learned, the greater the number of possibilities of seeing a situation under a description and perhaps the more effective the practitioner. Reflective teachers also would be able to describe situations under a variety of concepts. It is not enough just to have a repertoire of concepts. In order to formulate a problem, one must be able to use those concepts in making descriptions. Through practice and coaching, the teacher will have developed the ability to describe problematic situations in his or her own way. Finally, reflective teachers are able to trace the implications of seeing a problematic case under a particular description. Reflective practice requires that a description be affirmed and part of this affirmation is seeing that other aspects of the case are accounted for by the description that is chosen. That is, the implications of seeing the case under a description must be consistent with other features of the case that are known.

A second set of characteristics of reflective teachers relates to the second major aspect of reflective practice. Once a problem has been formulated, the teacher will need to experiment to determine whether the description should be accepted. Experimentation includes, it will be recalled, exploration, move testing and hypothesis testing; but I have maintained that for Schön there is no fundamental difference between the latter two. The first requirement for being a reflective teacher with respect to experimentation is to state a proposed move or hypothesis. Once a person has formed a hypothesis, it needs to be tested. In this case, the teacher must be able to bring about the state of affairs called for in the hypothesis. If it is proposed, for example, that a more concrete discussion of prejudice will result in a better understanding of the concept, the teacher must be able to effect the more concrete discussion. In general, the reflective teacher must be able to act on his intentions and to change situations. A reflective teacher will have a sense of judgment to determine whether an outcome is an affirmation or negation of the hypothesis. The teacher needs to be able to tell if his problem has been solved. To do this, he needs to determine if the outcome is indeed a result of his intervention, if the result is the one desired, and if other unintentional outcomes of his action are themselves desirable. This is a rather sophisticated judgment involving abilities to observe, to see the implications of a conceptual framework and to make appropriate judgments of value. This ability will be the culmination of all the other abilities so far identified, but it includes as well an understanding and appreciation of issues of value in teaching. If this is absent, the teacher's actions may well have negative or harmful effects on students.

The reflective teacher is, thus, one who, when faced with a problematic situation, can come to grips with the problem through bringing his knowledge and experience to bear on the problem. The result is that the teacher's beliefs and actions become subject to revision. In accepting many of Schön's criticisms, but in rejecting his claim to have provided an alternative epistemology, I have left unclear the logical nature of such revisions in belief and intention. I will consider this in detail in Chapter 7. Before moving on to these issues, there are other, quite different, proposals about the nature of theory and practice that need to be considered.

CHAPTER 4

Normative theory of education

The position that I will call "the normative theory of education" has been developed, or at least suggested, in a trilogy of articles by Paul Hirst.[1] The position has been developed, in large part, as a contrast to the views of O'Connor, discussed in Chapter 2, which claimed that educational theory is applied social science. Hirst's view is that educational theory cannot be restricted in this way. To be an adequate theory of education, it must bring all our knowledge of education to bear on practice. Although this view attempts to rectify the problems that can be attributed to scientific conceptions of educational theory, I want to claim that it is not an adequate account of the notions of educational theory and practice. I base this claim on two arguments: first, the position is not internally consistent; second, the account provides no clear and recognizable picture of what an educational theory is.

Normative educational theory

My first task, though, is to provide a description of the position I have chosen to call a normative educational theory. Hirst starts with O'Connor's two candidates for the definition of theory. O'Connor opted for defining "theory" as a set of logically interconnected hypotheses that have been confirmed by observation. The other definition, which O'Connor rejects and Hirst adopts, is that a theory is "a set or system of rules or a collection of precepts which guide or control actions of various kinds."[2] By adopting this broader definition, Hirst allows that educational theory contains much more than science; it will draw on "all the theoretical knowledge available in the social sciences. . . . But it also draws on history, philosophy and much else besides; all that is significant for the formulation and justification of its rational principles."[3] His reason for adopting the broader definition is that "ends and means are not ultimately separable."[4] Scientific conceptions of educational theory would place anything that is not scientific outside the bounds of educational theory. In that value claims, at least on their usual account, are not scientific; the goals towards which education should strive are outside the realm of educational theory when it is conceived in a scientific manner. Those who see educational theory in this way, of course, do not claim that debates about educational values and ends are not to be engaged in; rather, they claim that these debates fall outside the theory. This in no way deters from the ability of goals to provide direction for educational practice, for values can direct practice just as well from the outside. So, Hirst's rejection of the scientific view of educational theory cannot be based on the position that it does not include values and goals which are necessary for the direction of educational practice. Rather, his rejection of the scientific view of educational theory is based on a conceptual position about the relation of ends and means. Hirst must have a strong conception of what it means to say that ends and means are "not ultimately separable" in order for this to be the basis of his conception of educational theory. In order for this claim to provide such a base, we must see that for Hirst the relation between ends and means is a logical one. This would be the only kind of relation that would be strong enough, it seems, to warrant rejecting the scientific conception of educational theory.

This point is important because in basing his conception of educational theory on the claim that ends and means are not ultimately separable, Hirst has aligned himself with a particular philosophical position that is not without controversy, although the controversy itself cannot be dealt with here. It has been claimed by some that causes and their effects are logically independent of one another, in the sense that causes and effects can be specified without reference to the other, but that human actions and their reasons are not independent in this way. When the reason for a particular action is given the action is in effect being redescribed; we cannot understand what an action is independently of knowing what the reason for the action is. For example, we only understand that an educator's action is one of teaching multiplication by learning that the educator's reason for performing the action was to try to get the students to learn how to multiply. On the other hand, we can understand a particular event, such as a person deciding to become an educator, quite independently of knowing what caused the person to do this, whether the cause is seen in psychological, sociological or historical terms. In adopting this definition, Hirst has recast educational theory into a body of knowledge that deals with the actions of people. The scientific conception, which he rejects, deals with events or states of affairs and their causes. Educational theory now deals with what people do and their reasons for so doing; it also deals with them under a particular philosophical position regarding the relation of actions and reasons. Because reasons and actions are not, here, logically independent and because reasons for acting, unlike causes, are normative (and sometimes moral) claims, I have identified this position as normative educational theory.

One possible way to conceive educational theory (which Hirst used in his earlier articles but has rejected in the most recent) is to see educational theory as a combination of applied social science, applied history and applied philosophy. To construct an educational theory, one would take philosophy of education, history of education, educational psychology and sociology of education and apply their findings to educational practice. But even this collection may not be sufficient. Values and aims of education, which may not be included in any of these disciplines, would also be incorporated into the educational theory to provide direction to practice, but such values and aims would need independent justification before they could be included in a theory. An educational theory, then, would consist of claims justified by academic disciplines and would thereby provide rational principles of action for educational practice.

There are several problems with this way of conceiving educational theory. The first problem stems from the combination of disparate disciplines in an educational theory. The disciplines, to use Hirst's own account, are independent ways of coming to understand the world. As they have grown and become distinct, they have developed independent concepts, logics and truth tests.[5] Because, strictly speaking, the disciplines deal with different issues in different ways, there is no reason to suppose that when their results are put together they will speak to the practical issues at hand. In any discipline we are dealing with issues that are defined and conceived to some extent by the discipline itself. In philosophy, for example, questions are determined in part by the discipline. As an independent field of study, philosophy has its own existence in which people can participate. They do so, to some extent, on the field's terms. A person's own questions and concerns will have to be modified if they do not fit into the canons and constraints of the discipline.

The same is true of all the disciplines. Each has its own distinctive approach. These approaches will treat superficially similar questions in quite different ways. One need only to compare philosophical and sociological discussions of the notion of equality to see the different interests and ways of handling a question that exist in different disciplines. This means that if normative educational theory is the application of applied disciplines to practical issues, a theory would consist of a variety of independent findings that are based on their own sets of meanings and logics.

However, the practical issues with which such a theory is expected to deal would fall outside any of the disciplines. If they did not fall outside all disciplines, then one discipline would be able to deal with the issue and the need for a collection of disciplines would disappear. Since they fall outside of the disciplines it is not at all clear that the disciplines are able to deal with them. Disciplines provide explanations and justifications for phenomena that fall within their range of concern; they do not speak in any clear way to phenomena that are not in their purview. So if we accept Hirst's own account of the disciplines, we cannot make sense of how the disciplines can be collected together to provide direction and guidance to issues that are non-disciplinary.

A second problem is that a normative educational theory considered in this way is isolated from the realm of practice. If the rational principles of action that are to guide practice are derived from disciplines, then the principles are determined by the conceptual scheme of the relevant discipline; they are not determined by issues of practice. If an educational theory is to guide practice, the issues and problems that call for direction will be found in the realm of educational practice. The problems that need to be solved by an educational theory arise in the ordinary course of action in settings where teaching is taking place. They are defined by the practitioners who work at teaching and are trying to effect the education of others. Their concerns may not be those of scholars in the discipline. However, the definition of issues in this conception of educational theory must be that of the scholar and not necessarily of the practitioner. By starting from the point of view of the scholar, this construction of educational theory will result in theories of educational practice that take into account all of the knowledge of the discipline or disciplines but may not bear upon the work of the practitioner. So, even if it is possible to construct an educational theory in this way, there is no reason to believe that it will provide the guidance that the educational practitioner is seeking. For these reasons this particular way of viewing normative educational theory is to be rejected.

Problems of this sort are recognized by Hirst in the latest of his trilogy of articles. In order to overcome them, he now claims that an educational theory must begin with practice rather than the disciplines: "We must start from a consideration of current practice, the rules and principles that the practitioners employ in both characterizing that practice and deciding what ought to be done."[6] Such a characterization will set forth the beliefs and knowledge of practitioners in their language. The results of this activity will result in what he calls the practitioners' "operational educational theory."[7] The operational educational theory becomes the starting point for the development of the educational theory itself. The first sort of question that can be asked of an operational theory is whether "particular judgments or actions were the best that could be taken by this practitioner in the circumstances in which the situation arose."[8] At this level, the critical examination attempts to determine if in light of the practitioner's knowledge and beliefs the action was the most appropriate.

At a higher level of critical examination, the practitioner's knowledge and beliefs themselves become the subject of examination. Educational theory is centrally concerned with this level of examination because it is here that practical principles are determined to be rationally defensible. Hirst identifies two criteria for examination here. First, a practical principle must stand up to practical test.[9] Although Hirst has little to say about this criterion, the point, presumably, is that a sufficient condition for rejecting a practical principle would be its failure to bring about the desired result when it is tried in practice. If it is believed by some practitioner that showing films to students increases their interest in a subject but when the practitioner does show films and finds that the interest level is not changed, we have sufficient grounds for rejecting the original practical principle.

The second criterion is that practical principles must be justified in terms of correct knowledge and values. "If practical principles are to be rationally defensible they must therefore be seen to be formulated and tested in ways that incorporate wider beliefs and values that are rationally defensible rather than erroneous. In relation to practical affairs, therefore, it is the job of such disciplines as psychology, sociology and philosophy to provide a context of ever more rationally defensible beliefs and values for the development and practical testing of practical principles."[10] Hirst is not particularly clear on the role of this criterion. He does say that it will have to be utilized in an indirect way. He once held that rationally defensible practical principles would be derived from the disciplines. He now recognizes that such a view is mistaken, as I have already discussed, because philosophy is concerned with philosophical issues, not practical issues, psychology with psychological issues and so on. That is, from the disciplines one cannot derive statements that have applicability outside the discipline. So, practical principles cannot be shown to be justified by showing that they can be derived from the findings of the disciplines. In describing the indirect role of the disciplines, Hirst uses claims like "it is their job to aid these processes in every way possible"[11] and "in so far as they may suggest forms of practice. . . ."[12]

The position, then, of normative educational theory is that we start with actual practice and attempt to determine if what is actually done is rationally defensible. To make this judgment we have to determine if the practical principle can be tested in practice and if the principle is suggested by established conclusions of one or another of the disciplines. Such an activity will no doubt be complex because any given practical enterprise in schools will be such that many different disciplines will be suggested by the activity. Consider some activity that is designed to teach some element of mathematics to children. Without much effort one can see that value questions will be raised: Is it worth the children's time and effort to learn this? Philosophical questions arise: Will the teaching reflect the correct nature of mathematical knowledge? Psychological issues arise: Can these children learn this material? And sociological questions can be seen: What social end is served by these children learning this material? Since the disciplines are to aid in the formulation and testing of practical principles "in any way possible," all of these issues, and many others, will have to be considered to determine if the teaching of this particular element of mathematics is rationally defensible. The results of all these activities will be the normative educational theory that has been proposed.

A critique of normative educational theory

In this section I want to establish that while this view has much to teach us about the relation between theory and practice, this view of a normative educational theory is not a satisfactory resolution to the problem of stating the relation between theory and practice. The central problem that I see here is that the view is self-defeating. The position is correct, I believe, in locating the starting point for discussions of theory and practice in the realm of actual practice on the part of the practitioner. But, the conditions that are imposed on practice in order to generate a theory are such that no theory, or nothing recognizable as a theory, can result.

My discussion of this point will focus primarily on the second of the criteria that Hirst has established for a normative educational theory. The first criterion is that a practical principle must be subjected to practical test; the second is that a practical principle must receive support from the disciplines. The first point to notice is that what might be meant by this is not at all clear. Part of the reason is that the most obvious candidate for clarifying this relation is ruled out from the very start. If practical principles could be derived from the disciplines, or equivalently, are implied by statements in the disciplines, we would have a clear and unambiguous interpretation for the notion that the disciplines are to support practical principles. But this possibility is ruled out by Hirst. On his view of disciplinary knowledge, each discipline has a logic that makes it independent of other disciplines. This means that logical moves can never take one outside the discipline; but, of course, the realm of practice is outside any of the disciplines. So, it is impossible for practical statements to be derived from statements in any of the disciplines. Once, however, this point is recognized, Hirst is not able to give us any clear, alternative understanding of how disciplines and practice are related.

A number of suggestions for understanding this relation are given: "It is the job of [the] disciplines . . . to provide a context of ever more rationally defensible beliefs and values for the development . . . of practical principles"[13]; "It is the job [of the disciplines] to aid these processes [of the formulation and practical testing of practical principles] in every way possible"[14]; and, finally, "The knowledge, understanding, practical principles and forms of practical test which are thus appealed to incorporate and make use of elements that are open to rational criticism in various contributory disciplines."[15]

I want to suggest that once the relation of implication has been denied, there is no clear way to understand these claims. To use the third of the above claims, can practical principles incorporate beliefs from a discipline without being implied by them? On any plausible understanding of "incorporation" I should think not. Incorporation suggests class membership. If A can be incorporated into B then A is an instance of B; so A is implied by B or, alternatively, A can be derived from B. But this is precisely what is ruled out from the outset. So, using the notion of incorporation to describe the relation at hand does not seem to be very helpful.

Another possible interpretation given to us is that the disciplines provide a context for the practical principles in question. Presumably, a practical principle is supported to the degree that some discipline provides a context for the principle. The first suggestion here is that this means that the discipline incorporates the practical principle, a possibility that we have already seen has to be rejected given the prior elimination of any logical relation between disciplines and practice. An alternative would be to understand "providing a context" as giving background information. When we, for example, give the context in which a particular decision was made, we give such things as reasons for the need for the decision, the problem or issue that gave rise to the decision and the relevant factors or characteristics that were attended to in the making of the decision. In the case of a discipline providing a context for a practical principle, the only role for the discipline would seem to be that of providing relevant factors that need to be attended to. A teacher operates under the practical principle that one should move around the classroom as much as possible while teaching in order to prevent student misbehavior. One might claim, if we can assume that the research on teaching meets the requirements for disciplinary knowledge, that students in classrooms where the teacher moves around a good deal (that is, displays one aspect of what was earlier identified as "withitness") will tend to show greater academic achievement than students in classrooms where the teacher remains stationary in one spot in the room. This would seem to be a plausible candidate for a belief from a discipline providing a context for a practical principle. The discipline, while not implying the practical principle, does seem to provide some knowledge that can be attended to by the practitioner. But, the point of providing a context is to show, at least in part, that the practical principle is rationally defensible. It would seem that much more is required to make a practical principle rationally defensible than to be able to identify a bit of knowledge from some discipline that gives a factor that can be attended to in practice. In my example, the discipline relates moving about the classroom to academic achievement. In the practical principle there was no reference to such achievement; the teacher may well have adopted the practical principle for some other purpose such as to provide variety in the teacher's routine. If this is the case, then the discipline while still providing a context into which the principle can be placed does not provide a rational defense for the teacher's action. To put the point in a somewhat different light, suppose now that the teacher has the practical principle that one should move about the classroom while teaching in order to increase academic achievement. Now let us appeal, for the sake of argument, to the "well-established value" in philosophy of education that a teacher ought to promote academic achievement. This, too, provides a context for the practical principle, but does not provide a rational defense for it. The discipline tells us that academic achievement is a factor that needs attention in teaching, but it does not defend the claim that teachers should be moving about the room while teaching. We do, however, get a rational defense for the practical principle that teachers should move about the classroom in order to increase academic achievement if we combine the "finding" from research on teaching that moving about the classroom tends to increase academic achievement and the "finding" from philosophy of education that academic achievement ought to be encouraged. The problem is that we also get a valid deductive argument in which the practical principle is the conclusion. But, this is precisely what is ruled out. The notion of rational defense explicitly excludes the logical derivation of practical principles from the disciplines. It seems, in conclusion, that although we can make sense of the notion that the disciplines provide a context for practical principles, they do not provide a rational defense for them. In order to get a rational defense, it seems we have to invoke notions of logical derivation which were excluded at the outset on other grounds.

The third and final way in which Hirst describes the relation between the disciplines and practical principles is that the disciplines aid the formulation and practical testing of practical principles in every way possible. I submit that this formulation is too vague to provide any help in understanding the relation between principles of action and disciplinary knowledge. "Every way possible" allows any relation whatsoever; it must include the already excluded possibility that a discipline can aid the formulation of practical principles by being the premises of valid deductive arguments of which practical principles are the conclusion. Hirst seems to be overstating his point here, and the more specific, but unsatisfactory, interpretations that have been considered must be regarded as giving his point.

Hirst has rejected his own earlier formulations of the relation between theory and practice on the basis that the disciplined bases of theory prevent any connection with practice. That is, on his own account of what constitutes a discipline, the questions that a theory considers are formulated within the parameters set by the discipline. Because the issues of practice fall outside any discipline, a theory must address questions other than those raised by practice. In the most recent version of his position, he has recognized this issue, but the argument of this section has been to suggest that he has not solved it. It still seems that his acceptance of the logical independence of the various disciplines prevents them from dealing with issues of practice. Even if we start from practical questions and formulate the practitioner's response to them as an "operational educational theory," when we try to move to a normative theory of education we still have to translate the practical issues into psychological, sociological, philosophical or historical issues. Given that the latter sorts of issues are discipline-based, and so are independent of practice, we need some basis for making the translation, a dictionary if you will, that enables us to move from the practical to the disciplines. It is just this dictionary that still eludes Hirst.

Another way of showing the problem is to note Hirst's reliance on the notion of theory or disciplines making practical claims "rationally defensible." This, it seems to me, is as close as he comes to stating the relation between theory and practice or providing that basis for the translation from practical questions to theoretical ones. But what is packed into this notion is not at all clear.

As Hirst does not make clear what is meant by "rationally defensible," a number of candidates need to be considered. If a theory shows that a statement of practice is true, then we would say that it shows it to be rationally defensible; so, I will take this as the first candidate. If a theory shows a statement to be true, that means that a sound argument could be constructed with the premises consisting of theoretical statements and the conclusion being the statement of practice. But on his own account, each theoretical discipline has its logic. Given this, the conclusion of an argument must belong to the same discipline as its premises. So here, again, we have the boundary between the disciplines and practice being crossed in a way Hirst denies is possible. This candidate cannot be what is meant by being rationally defensible.

A second candidate is to take the somewhat weaker notion that a theory justifies belief in the practical statement. This too seems to be a reasonable candidate, for if a theory shows that one is justified in believing a particular practical claim it seems plausible to say that we have a rational defense for the claim. Again Hirst's account of disciplines seems to put in doubt whether this is a viable candidate. As disciplines have their own logics and sets of concepts it is difficult to see how they can warrant belief in claims that share neither their logics nor concepts. The difficulty is seen quite clearly when one looks to see whether one discipline can warrant belief in a claim in another discipline. No amount of philosophical statements will warrant belief in a particular sociological or psychological claim. What warrants belief in social scientific claims is the evidence for that claim, and what counts as evidence is defined by that discipline. Evidence does not seem to be able to cross the boundary lines between disciplines. The same difficulty holds where the claim to be rationally defended belongs to no discipline, as in the case of practical claims. Since the concept of evidence itself is relative to a discipline, the evidence for a practical claim will belong to the same discipline as the claim. As the claim itself belongs to no discipline, so will the evidence. So, providing grounds for believing a claim is not a satisfactory interpretation for what might be meant by "rationally defensible."

A third candidate is to say that a practical claim is made rationally defensible by a theory if the theory provides an efficacious justification for the practical claim or, in rather more straightforward language, the theory explains why the practice works. A particular social practice might be said to be rationally defensible in this sense if a particular sociological theory shows that the practice is functional. Similarly, a teaching practice may be said to be rationally defensible if one can produce a theory to explain why the practice works. There are two sorts of issues about this interpretation that raise questions about its acceptability. First, if we accept the interpretation, there are questions that must be asked about the theory that is invoked. A practice will not be rationally defensible if the theory that accounts for the practice is not itself adequate or acceptable. Bad theory cannot make a practice defensible. So the original interpretation must be modified to say that a practice can be rationally defended if there is an adequate theory that explains the practice.

Casting the position in this way leads to the second issue concerning this interpretation. What this interpretation requires is a kind of causal explanation. To explain why something works is to give an account of how the practice produces the desired effect. If an action is regarded as being efficacious, it is held that the action brings about the desired result. How the theory provides such an account is not at issue here; my point is that the question at hand presupposes a certain kind of explanation. This presupposition does present difficulties for Hirst's account. In his understanding of disciplines, causal explanations are typical of only one discipline: science. It is in the natural and social sciences, including, of course, psychology and sociology, that we find causal explanations. So, if we interpret being rationally defensible as providing an account of why a practice works, we need only one discipline to provide the theoretical basis for practice. This goes against his explicit requirement that a theory of education must be multidisciplinary or interdisciplinary. The third candidate for interpreting "rationally defensible" then is not suitable. Although it sounds plausible to say that a theory makes a practical claim "rationally defensible," once we try to give a more precise interpretation to this phrase, we see that Hirst's conceptions of theory and discipline prevent us from finding an adequate meaning for this notion.[16]

In summary, as long as Hirst maintains the logical independence and exclusivity of disciplines, the way is blocked for providing an adequate account for the relation of theory and practice. Although he has recognized many of the problems that his original account raised, the commitments he brings to his latest formulation of the issues prevent him from coming to an acceptable account of how the various theories that relate to education can provide a basis for our practical knowledge of what happens in teaching.

Recognizing an educational theory

So far in my discussion of a normative theory of education I have focused on questions of its internal consistency. Now I would like to consider another kind of question: would such a theory, if one could be constructed, serve any purpose? This is a rather more general, and even more nebulous, question. A theory, in general, can serve many kinds of purposes: those of understanding, control, explanation, knowledge, as well as of a variety of other concerns that would not seem to be central (such as to show one's authority or even erudition). A theory can probably serve as many purposes as there are people who use the theory. In spite of the vagueness of my question, I wish to pursue this line because of my suspicion that even if a normative theory of education could be developed, we probably would not recognize one if presented to us and would not know what to do with it once it was pointed out to us.

What is typically characteristic of theories in general is that they are concerned with a particular issue or topic and utilize a relatively restricted range of procedures to provide an account for the topic. Whether we look at science (the theory of special relativity), at politics (the Marxist theory of the state) or at philosophy (the correspondence theory of truth), we see that a theory picks out a special topic or range of phenomena for consideration. There are, of course, exceptions; we can find many cases where what is cited as a theory does not identify any specific topic as its subject, as in Aristotle's theory of science or Plato's theory of education. But, even here the label assigned to the theory gives us a starting point for considering what the theory is about; it helps us, for example, in deciding which parts of Plato's work are not relevant, or less relevant, to his understanding of education. Also, it seems typical that a theory has a relatively restricted range of procedures that one needs to know in order to be able to use the theory. One can see this by thinking about what one needs to learn to be able to do before one can set about to learn or use the theory. This is not to say that the required knowledge is straightforward or easily acquired; rather, associated with a theory is a relatively specific set of knowledge and skills. If one wants to learn the theory of special relativity, which is no mean feat, one at least knows where to begin. Also, one knows that many kinds of learning are not needed for the particular goal; one knows at the outset of learning this theory that a knowledge of how to conjugate French verbs will not be needed. So, in typical cases when we want to study a theory, we know that it will be about a relatively particular set of issues and that a relatively specific set of procedures, skills and background knowledge will be utilized in the theory.

However, none of this seems to be true of a normative theory of education. Although the theory is ostensibly about education, the development of the theory is such that no limit is placed on what a theory might involve. The starting points for normative educational theory are the claims that practitioners have discovered that work, the operational educational theory. This limits the theory to the general realm of what goes on in schools or other educational contexts, but within this realm there are an endless range of claims that the theory is expected to incorporate. Suppose a teacher has learned from practice that moving about the classroom helps to keep students attentive, that the same instruction in reading is more effective with girls than with boys and that all students should learn to speak at least one other language besides their native tongue. A normative theory is expected to account for all of this as well as any other practical claims that might be found to work. One is hard pressed to see how all this can be combined into a coherent whole. The kind of unity that is afforded to theories by the focus of their subject matters is quite obviously absent here. As well, there is no set of procedures that is distinctively appropriate to a normative theory of education. By the definition of such a theory, any disciplinary approach can be used in developing a normative theory of education. The theory itself gives no ground for believing that any possible mode of inquiry is irrelevant; one cannot even say that a knowledge of the conjugation of French verbs will not be needed.

What we are presented with in this conceptualization of a normative theory of education seems, then, to give no clear picture of what such a theory would be like if we were to find one. It can deal with anything we want, in any way we want. The notion is so open that anything, and nothing, would seem to fit the bill. A conception that is this broad in its formulation would seem, I submit, to be of little use.

CHAPTER 5

Theory of practice

Yet another approach to the question of the relation of theory and practice is to use the nature of practice as the starting point and develop a theory that recognizes the distinctive nature of practice. There are many ways in which this task can be conceived; the approach that I will consider is that recommended by Donna Kerr in "The Structure of Quality in Teaching."[1] Kerr is concerned primarily with developing a theory of teaching that allows us to make judgments of quality, i.e., evaluations, of particular teaching episodes. In doing this, she describes what she calls a theory of practice. It is this aspect of her work that I will discuss. Pointing out Kerr's main concern in this work may help to clarify why a theory of practice is both important and different from the candidates we have so far examined. Kerr suggests that a broader and more comprehensive theory of teaching is needed to allow us to make appropriate judgments about the quality of teaching. The candidates we are offered in the educational research literature, particularly that research that deals, in a self-described way, with "effective teaching," are not up to the task because the way in which teaching is conceptualized in these studies is inadequate. Teaching is seen in these studies as a kind of empirical phenomenon which can be studied through the procedures and canons of empirical science. Kerr's objection is that teaching, as a species of practice, must be conceived in a different way and, therefore, studied in a different way. This kind of study will further allow us to make informed judgments about the quality of teaching, or to use the current jargon, we will have a better understanding of what effective teaching is.

It is not my concern to examine the analysis of teaching that Kerr provides. Rather, I want to discuss what she says about the nature of a theory of practice to see if it will provide a firm footing for discussions of the relation of theory and practice. To anticipate, I will argue that this conception of a theory of practice does not meet the requirements held for it, but that it does provide a major step in understanding the relation of theory and practice.

Let me turn, then, to Kerr's views on what a theory of practice is. It is, first, to be distinguished from a theory of phenomena. A theory of practice is concerned with quality; a theory of phenomena with prediction.

The point of theory of practice (or a practical activity) is to augment our understanding of that practice for purposes of improving the actions that constitute the practice. While the central test of theory of phenomena might be writ narrow as a standard of predictive efficacy . . . , the base-line test of theory of practice must be cast as a standard of quality, where the criteria of quality in some way include but are not limited to considerations of efficacy. From theory of practice, then, we should await a framework for identifying the ways in which teaching actions can succeed (or fail).[2]

This identifies what seems to be the crucial difference for Kerr between the two kinds of theory; there are as well several similarities. The first is that both theories of practice and theories of phenomena will describe the topic under consideration. There are, though, different ways in which a topic can be described. A theory of phenomena will describe the relevant phenomena in some kind of observational language. A theory of practice must use action language, rather than observational language, to describe the practice under consideration. Practices such as teaching are comprised of actions, things that people do intentionally or purposefully. If we describe an action in observational language, as we can, we lose its intentional nature. To use a simple example, when we describe a person's wave in observational language, as a movement of the arm, we no longer have in the description the fact that the wave was intended as a signal of some sort from one person to another. To describe the movement in action language, as a wave, is to show that the movement is intentional and purposive. What makes the movement a wave is the intention or purpose behind it; the observable movements do not make it a wave. If our concern is the practice of waving, we will, then, need to describe it in the language that shows it to be a wave. Hence, if we are concerned with practices, we will have to describe the practice in action language. An observational language will not describe the events under consideration.

The next step in Kerr's analysis of a theory of practice is not immediately clear to me. Working in the context of developing a theory of teaching, she wants to identify "the quality structure of teaching as part of theory of practice."[3] Just what is meant by "quality structure" is not made clear, but it does seem to be a notion that is applicable in general to theories of practice and not just to this theory of teaching. She develops this point by going to her analysis of action where she reminds us that actions can be described in different ways, and it is this that allows us to evaluate actions. This possibility of evaluation is what provides, it seems, the quality structure. About the possibility of describing actions in different ways she ways, "We can describe whether what [person] *m* does under one description (*b*) is adequate for what he wants to do under the more general description (*a*). Thus, we can evaluate *m*'s doing of *a*."[4] Her example may help to clarify the claim. It is conceivable that one could choose a textbook for a course by flipping a coin. So, in this case a more general description of the action of flipping a coin would be choosing a textbook. To evaluate the person's choosing of the textbook, we can ask whether the flipping of a coin is adequate for the choosing of a textbook. This point is generalizable to practices other than teaching. To revert to the example of waving, a person can wave to another for the purpose of warning him, say, of oncoming traffic. So, the wave can also be described as a warning of an approaching vehicle. We can evaluate the action by asking if the wave is adequate to serve as such a warning.

It is clear that for the theory to have any substance, this notion of adequacy must be spelled out in more detail. Kerr does this by giving two general tests of adequacy.

> The first, the test of *subjective adequacy,* queries whether *m*'s action *b* fits *m*'s relevant beliefs and values. . . . The second test features *objective adequacy.* While *m* might believe that what he is doing (*b*) is adequate for . . . (*a*), what he is doing may not be adequate for *a* on standards either of the knowledge community or of the moral and political context, or of both.[5]

What must be done now in any theory of practice is to specify what the relevant beliefs and values are in the realm of discourse of the theory. The bulk of Kerr's article is a discussion of the beliefs and values that are relevant to an understanding of teaching, which are not my concern at present. In general, though, one can say that the most difficult and most crucial task in the construction of a theory of practice along Kerr's model will be the analysis which produces the beliefs and values that are relevant to an area of action.

In sum, then, a theory of practice will consist of two parts. First, it will provide a description in action language of the events or topics to be made understandable by the theory. Second, it will contain criteria for evaluating actions. These criteria will be the beliefs and values that determine either subjectively or objectively whether an action which is performed is adequate for achieving the action under a more general description. I now want to consider whether this approach is sound.

I will consider the merits of this account by examining two claims made of a theory of practice: that it is predictive and that it provides understanding. It is stated that a theory of practice must meet the same requirements that a theory of empirical phenomena must meet. To repeat the relevant quotation,

> While the central test of theory of phenomena might be writ narrow as a standard of predictive efficacy . . . , the base-line test of theory of practice must be cast as a standard of quality where the criteria of quality in some way include but are not limited to considerations of efficacy.[6]

While the second occurrence of the word "efficacy" is not modified by "predictive" one assumes that it is to be so understood. The claim here is that a theory of practice, like a theory of empirical phenomena, must provide the basis for making predictions. An empirical theory provides the basis for making predictions by formulating general laws or regularities that enable one to infer from a set of initial conditions to the occurrence of an event. The occurrence of, say, a solar eclipse can be predicted on the basis of the knowledge of the laws or, at least, regularities that govern planetary motion and from the present positions of the Earth, Moon and Sun. What in a theory of practice will provide the basis for predicting events?

There are two components of a theory of practice that might answer this question. The first is to look at the descriptive component; a theory of practice must be able to describe the events under consideration. But descriptions do not enable one to make predictions. A description of a teaching episode would not seem to enable one to make any substantive predictions about teaching. One sort of prediction does seem possible, but it is essentially a trivial prediction. A person who learns a description of some action will learn how to describe that action. This would seem to enable the person to be able to recognize future instances of that action, or, in other words, it enables us to predict that if the person sees another case of teaching, it will be described as a case of teaching. That is, learning descriptions may enable us to make predictions about the future language use of the person who learned the description; it would not seem to enable us to make any predictions about the action itself.

It will be countered that the descriptions in a theory of practice are unlike those in empirical theories. In an empirical theory, the language is that of regularities and general laws. In a theory of practice, the language is action language. Does the use of action language enable predictions? To say that a person does something as an action is to say, roughly, that the action is intended to bring about some goal or purpose. Knowing that a person has an intention would seem to enable us to predict that, other things being equal, the person will do something to bring about the intention, but we would need a great deal of knowledge about the person's beliefs in order to predict what the person will do to bring about the intention. To know that the person is a teacher, for example, enables us to predict that, other things being equal, something will be done to help others learn; but this is all that can be predicted. From the fact that the event is an action, nothing further can be determined without a great deal of information about the person.

Full knowledge of the person's action would not seem to provide the basis for prediction for a quite different reason. The analysis of action that is used here gives six conditions for action: "m does a, only if (a) m intends a; (b) a happens; (c) m does b; (d) b is adequate for a; (e) m believes that b is adequate for a; (f) m does b because m intends a."[7]

Although this provides an analysis for a person doing something, it does not provide the basis for making predictions. The only evidence that we have for the parts of the analysis is that the action was performed. That is, it is the performance of the action that tells us that *b* is adequate for *a*, that the person believed it was adequate and that the person did it because *a* was intended. The analysis can be used to explain something as an action; it cannot be used to predict the occurrence of possible actions.

We can also ask if the other component of a theory of practice provides the basis for prediction. A theory of practice provides a set of relevant beliefs and values that enable one to make evaluations. The relevant beliefs and values that are employed would seem to be the result of some sort of conceptual analysis. In the example that Kerr provides, a theory of teaching, the relevant beliefs and values are determined by analyzing the nature of teaching to see what considerations are necessary to understand our concept of teaching. She seeks to provide those aspects of the practice that are necessary to any particular instance of teaching. Contingent aspects of teaching would not seem to be relevant to an evaluation of the practice of teaching. We use the nature of the subject matter being taught as providing a basis for evaluating teaching because it is necessary to teaching that some subject matter be taught. We do not use the sex of the teacher as a basis for evaluating teaching because this is only contingently related to teaching; it is not necessary for a person to be male or to be female in order to teach.

This would seem to be a general feature of practice. Any evaluation of a practice that drew only on contingent facts of the practice would be inadequate as an evaluation. Such a claim would not serve as a recommendation for improvement of the practice because future instances of the practice might not include the contingent aspect that was identified. It would not serve as an evaluation of a practice if the characteristic identified in the evaluation did not matter to the practice. To criticize a teaching performance on the basis of the teacher's hair color would seem to be an inadequate evaluation because changing the teacher's hair color would not seem to have any bearing on changing the teacher's performance. We can say this because we know that hair color is a contingent fact of teachers and teaching.

We separate contingent and necessary features of a practice through conceptual analysis of the practice. It is our conceptual understanding of teaching that tells us that hair color is not a necessary feature of teaching. We do not learn this by observation or generalizations from experience. So, the second component of a theory of practice presupposes that conceptual analysis has been done; it does not require that any observational or scientific work has been done.

By identifying necessary features of a practice, this sort of analysis will not provide the basis for making predictions about what might happen. The most that they might do is to make it possible to make recommendations about how the practice might or should proceed, which after all is precisely their role in this conception of theory of practice. An example will help to show the point. One of the relevant beliefs and values that Kerr identifies in her theory of teaching is the nature of subject matter. "The quality of one's teaching depends in important part upon one's understanding the subject well enough both to choose appropriate learnings and to design plans that do not violate the nature of the subject matter."[8] This does not give us a basis for predicting what teaching actions will take place. Rather it provides a basis for making suggestions or recommendations as to how the teaching might go or should proceed. Even if a teacher accepts the principle that good teaching should not violate the nature of subject matter, we do not have a basis for predicting what that teacher will do. Not only is there a wide range of other factors that the teacher must take into account, more importantly, there would seem to be an indefinite number of teaching activities that respect the nature of any particular subject matter. We cannot use this principle to tell what a teacher will do; the principle works to tell us whether what a teacher has done is appropriate. Once a teaching act is before us we can use the principle to criticize the act for not representing appropriately the nature of the subject matter or we can commend the act for doing so. But, it is not possible to use the principle to predict what a teacher will do. This fits entirely with Kerr's concern; a theory of practice is to provide the means for distinguishing quality performances and the notion of relevant beliefs and values was introduced in order to make judgments of the adequacy of performances.

Each of the components, then, of a theory of practice is not capable of providing the basis for making predictions. It is not clear, as a result, how a theory of practice is to be efficacious in making predictions as Kerr claims it should be. It should be noted that this alleged characteristic of theory of practice is not central to this kind of theory. Providing the basis for making predictions is claimed to be a characteristic that theories of practice share with theories of empirical phenomena. I have tried to suggest that this formulation of a theory of practice does not provide the basis for making predictions. This result is not, I think, very troubling because it is not clear to me why such a theory should be able to make predictions. A theory of practice, as Kerr states, is to provide a basis for identifying quality. Its concern is with improving performance. If the improvement of performance is what is important, we are not particularly interested in predicting what will happen. Instead, we are interested in making things better; this interest, it seems, makes prediction a relatively unimportant consideration. In an empirical theory, we are concerned to be able to say such things as "At time t event x will occur." In a theory of practice that strives to improve practice, we want to say, "If a good performance is to occur at time t, then x, y and z should be done." So, it is not clear why the notion of prediction is seen to be so central to the notion of a theory of practice.

The second claim that is made for theory of practice is that it "provides a means for understanding."[9] There is no doubt that this is central to a theory of practice. If we are to use a theory to provide evaluations of and recommendations for actions, the theory must enable us to understand the practice at hand. Surely, one hopes that the judgments of quality that are made will flow from an understanding of the practice. I now want to consider the question of whether the theory as it is conceived provides a means for understanding. Again, I will do this by considering the two components of theory of practice that Kerr identifies: providing descriptions and providing the basis for evaluations.

A theory of practice provides a description in action language of the practice at hand. Can such a description provide a means for understanding? It would appear not, at least in the sense one expects from a theory. A description explains nothing. To describe a child's learning difficulties does not explain why he has difficulty in learning. To describe a child's network of friends does not explain why she is friendly with these particular children. To describe a practice does not tell us how the practice came into being, why it is performed, what end or ends it might serve, or any of the other things that would contribute to our understanding of the practice. A description would serve, however, to enable one to know what the practice is and to identify or recognize instances of it. These may represent the beginnings of understanding; a first step in understanding something may well be the ability to recognize it. But, they are not sufficient to serve as a theoretical understanding of the practice. We would not attribute to a person a theoretical understanding of a practice if all she were able to do was to recognize instances of the practice.

Again, the fact that a description in a theory of practice is expressed in action language needs special attention for it may be claimed that action language explains as well as describes. To describe an action is to give the intention under which it is performed. The intention of the action is part of the description. When we describe the movement of a person's arm, for example, as a wave we have moved from behavioral language to action language, but to describe the movement as a wave is to identify the intention of the action. In describing the action as a wave we know the person's intention in performing the action, in this case to show recognition, and we understand why the action was performed. In action language, to know an intention (which is part of the description of the action) is to understand the action. Once we see what a person is doing as being a case of the action of teaching, we understand what the person is doing. Can it be said, then, that because the description is in action language, the descriptive component is sufficient to provide the means for understanding that we expect from a theory?

I want to claim that it does not because although knowing the intention behind an action provides an understanding of an action, it does not provide a means for understanding a practice. Let me, first, try to exemplify this point by means of a simple and perhaps trivial case. Consider the practice of knot tying. The sheepshank is a knot that provides a secure way of shortening a rope without cutting it. A person who performs the action of tying a sheepshank intends, then, to shorten the rope. The knowledge of the person's intention is sufficient to understand the particular action, but it does not enable us to understand the practice of knot tying. In order to understand the practice, we would need to know, besides the intentions of the actors, a bit of cultural history and some simple science at the very least. The practice of knot tying, it seems to me, is not understood unless we know something about friction and how it works to keep knots tied and unless we know something about how rope became so important in certain cultures. There is probably much more to be learned here; a student of knots would be able to identify many more areas of concern.

But, this is sufficient to make my point. A practice is a composite of activities. Action language may be sufficient to understand individual actions, but it is the fallacy of composition to infer that what explains actions also explains practices. Knowing intentions may explain an action, but we cannot conclude from this that knowing intentions explains the practice of which the action is a part. From simple practices, like tying knots, to complex ones, like teaching, knowing the intentions of the agents is only part of understanding the practice. In order to understand the practice itself, though, we have to investigate many other kinds of questions besides what the intentions are in the performance of individual actions. So, I conclude that the descriptive component of a theory of practice does not provide the means for understanding.

I must now consider whether the other component, the evaluative component, provides a means for understanding a practice. I will, again, try to show my point by means of the simple case of knot tying. A theory of the practice of knot tying would have to provide a set of relevant beliefs and values that are central to the practice that would serve as standards for judging whether particular actions are adequate for the intentions they are to serve. Suppose, further, that in this case the relevant beliefs and values are presented to us with the practice; that is, that we do not have to engage in the kind of conceptual analysis that Kerr, for example, does in identifying the relevant beliefs and values for the practice of teaching. Here, one has all the requirements for the theory, but does one have the means for providing an understanding of the practice?

To carry the case further, suppose that among the relevant beliefs and values for knot tying is the principle that knots should not come undone of their own accord. In a specific case of knot tying, in an attempt to secure a package for mailing, a person ties a granny knot. It is the case that a granny knot is a less reliable knot, in the sense that it is more likely to come undone, than the similar square knot. So, the theory of the practice of knot tying tells us that the granny knot is not the one to be used in this case, and further the theory gives grounds for improving the practice of knot tying. This homely example fits Kerr's account of a theory of practice, but we seem to be no closer to an understanding of the practice of tying knots.

Knowing the rules for knot tying, and even being able to give reliable judgments on knots, surely are part of understanding the practice. But, it does seem to be the case that we would identify a person who can do this to be a theoretician, or one who has a theory of practice. The reason for this is that the person in this case has not had to think about or reflect on the rules of the practice; a condition of the example was that the rules for tying knots were presented as given. The person only had to apply the rules. Similarly, while we are glad that a child is able to apply and follow the rules of morality, we would not say that the child had developed a theory of ethical behavior. The problem here seems to reside in the way the person comes to have the relevant beliefs and values; a question on which Kerr is silent. Being able to make judgments of quality does not make the person a theoretician of practice. Instead, it seems that it is the doing of the conceptual analysis that develops the rules to be used in making judgments of quality that makes the person a theoretician of practice. This is seen in Kerr's own case where it is the analysis of teaching that she does that provides the understanding of teaching. This analysis is not included as a component of a theory of practice; rather, its results are included in the theory. It seems that the relevant beliefs and values are developed independently of the theory and then are included in it. The force of my example is to show that it is the activity of determining the relevant beliefs and values that contributes to understanding. If we take a set of such beliefs and values independently of their development and place them in a theory we do not achieve understanding. I want, then, to claim that it is not the theory as conceived that provides understanding; it is the reflection and revision to one's beliefs that are preparatory to the theory that provide the understanding.

One wants to object that this is carrying distinctions to a ridiculous level. How can an activity produce understanding and the results of the activity not? The point here is that one can learn the results or outcomes of an activity in a variety of ways, some of which may not show understanding. One can, for example, memorize the results of mathematical theorems; alternatively one can learn to prove mathematical theorems. There is a sense in which we can say that each person knows the same things, and each of them may be equally adept in applying the theorems. But, we want to say that the person who can prove mathematical theorems, rather than the one who can recite them from memory, has the better understanding of mathematics. This is the person who sees the derivation of the theorem, can explain why it is true and can relate it to the realm of mathematics. A different kind of learning takes place when one learns how to do an activity than when one simply learns the results of the activity. It is the learning of how to do the activity that is crucial for the understanding of a practice.

The upshot of this discussion is that it is the conceptual analysis[10] of the practice to determine its necessary features that provides the means for understanding the practice. It is not the description of the practice or the evaluation of actions within in the practice that provides for understanding. Kerr has drawn our attention to an aspect of the relation of theory and practice that has received little attention. Conceptual analysis to find necessary conditions is an activity most closely associated with philosophy. The lesson I find here is that theoretical understanding of a practice turns out to be, to a great extent, a philosophical activity. It cannot be solely a philosophical activity. Understanding a practice will still require empirical knowledge and value commitments. But philosophy has become important to the question of how theory and practice are related in a way not generally realized.

CHAPTER 6

The nature of teaching

The positions considered so far have been attempts to provide an understanding of theory and practice in education that start from accounts of the nature of theory and practice. I have tried to show that such attempts have been unsuccessful in that the results of these discussions have not captured what is necessary in understanding the activity of teaching or in providing direction for teacher education. The common difficulty that these positions face stems from the fact that they begin from a characterization of theory and practice, not from a characterization of teaching, the phenomenon the theories purport to explain. The position that I want to develop will begin with an account of teaching in this chapter and then move to questions of theory and practice in the next. In approaching the problem in this way I hope that the resulting account of theory and practice will be grounded in the reality of the phenomenon being explained.

To begin this effort I will now turn to the activity of teaching. The characterization of teaching that will be useful for my purposes is a clarification of its essential features, those features that make an activity a teaching activity. When looking for such necessary features or conditions, a philosophical analysis is the approach best suited for achieving the purpose. At this point, the empirical truths and contingencies of teaching are not going to provide direction to the discussion. Although many important and insightful factual discoveries have been made about teaching through research on teaching and schools, what is needed for understanding the relation of theory and practice in teacher education is an understanding at a basic level of the nature of teaching. In doing so, I will provide an account of the philosophically important features of teaching; I will not attempt to provide a definition of the term "teaching."[1]

Teaching as an intentional activity

It is, I think, a commonplace in the philosophical literature on teaching to say that teaching is an intentional activity. When someone is teaching, he or she has the purpose, goal or intention of getting someone to learn something.[2] The existence of a relation between the activity of teaching and the intention of getting someone to learn something is, of course, much more than an empirical generalization on instances of teaching. That trying to achieve learning is the purpose of teaching is not something one comes to see as a result of looking at large numbers of examples of teaching. It is, rather, part of what we mean by teaching. It is not something we discover about teaching; it is the principal criterion that we use to identify actions as teaching actions. When faced with the question of determining whether an action is a teaching action, as opposed to some other kind of action such as reciting, talking or acting in a play, it is the intention of bringing about learning that is the basis for distinguishing teaching from other activities. The observable behaviors in which a teacher, reciter and actor engage may be indistinguishable. What entitles us to distinguish among them is the intention that each serves. The intention the activity serves, then, is a part of the meaning of the concept, and not a factual discovery one makes about the activity.

That the intention of teaching provides a criterion for the use of the concept can be seen by noting that it is inconceivable, or at best odd, to say that a person is teaching but has no intention that someone else learn something. It is inconceivable because, if we have a case where someone claims to be teaching but says that he has no intention or concern that someone learns something, we would say that the person is contradicting himself. To claim to teach without intending that someone else learn is to claim nothing. In a literal way we do not know what to make of such a claim; because of this, the intention that someone learn something is a necessary condition for an activity to be a teaching activity.

Although it makes no sense to talk of teaching without the intention to bring about learning, our response to cases of people who report that they are teaching but not intending that anyone learn is the same as our response when faced with any statement that makes no sense; we try to give it some sense. When a person says that he is teaching, for example, but could care less whether anyone learns, our response may be not to accuse the person of self-contradiction; rather we seek some way, perhaps a metaphorical way, in which we can make sense out of the person's apparently odd claim. Here, we might want to say that the person is going through the motions of doing what would be appropriate to enable someone else to learn, but due to frustration, lack of care or lack of energy, the person is not sincere in trying to get the others to learn. Another interpretation of the claim that a person is teaching without intending that others learn would be that the person does not realize that what she is doing will result in learning on the part of others. It may be said of a parent, for example, that her actions teach a child the importance of sharing even though her intention was to stop a dispute between the child and another. Here, the parent's actions are consistent with those that would be performed if the parent had the actual intention of bringing about this learning. Because of this we can extend the notion of teaching metaphorically to cover this sort of case. The intention to bring about learning is, thus, a necessary condition for central cases of the use of the concept of teaching. However, like all concepts, there are extensions and metaphorical uses of the concept. These extensions of the concept rely on the central use to give them their meaning; they are close enough to the central uses that we can see how they resemble cases where the intention is to bring about learning.

Another kind of problematic case stems from the fact that a single action can be done for more than one purpose or from more than one intention. In such cases, an action may be correctly described in more than one way. As a result, the kinds of distinctions we see between teaching and other activities may seem to fall apart. An earlier example contrasted acting in a play with teaching. But playwrights may, and often do, have the intention of using their work as a means of getting others to learn; there is, after all, didactic drama. In such cases, an actor committed to the message of the play may fairly be said to be teaching as well as acting in a performance of the play. The actor is portraying the character as well as trying to get his audience to learn. In such a case, one can say that he is both acting and teaching. In this way, a person's action can be seen under several descriptions. Teaching actions can often be accurately described as other actions as well.

To characterize teaching as those actions that intend to bring about learning does not distinguish the many kinds of actions that can fulfill this intention. That is to say, the account given here allows for many kinds of approaches to teaching that in other circumstances or for other purposes may be questionable. Activities as diverse as lecturing and demonstrating, instructing and correcting, indoctrinating and reasoning, conditioning and encouraging may all be done with the intention of getting someone else to learn something. As a result, all can be examples of teaching. In this way, teaching is seen to be a family of related activities, related by intention rather than behavior. In developing a theory of teaching or of education, the distinctions between these activities would become very important. Moral considerations might enter to rule out, say, indoctrination. Empirical considerations might be used to claim that demonstrating is more effective than lecturing. For my concern here, it is the family resemblance that is important rather than the differences within the family. So, teaching will be considered in this broad way as including all of these activities.

Teaching as an intentional situation

I hope that all of this is uncontroversial. To say that teaching activities are characterized by the intention which they serve is a straightforward way of distinguishing these activities from others. What is less obvious and more controversial is the implication that I want to draw from this benign starting point. The intentions which characterize teaching activities create what I want to call "intentional situations."[3] An intention is what I have argued makes an activity a teaching activity. The teacher in a classroom has the intention that the students will learn something; the teacher as well determines what is to be learned. Of course, not everything that a teacher does in a classroom is intended to bring about some learning in the students, but this is to say nothing more than that not everything a teacher does is teaching. On the other hand, people other than professional teachers may engage in teaching activities. A day-care center worker, for example, may operate under the general intention of seeking to insure the welfare of those in the day-care center, but from time to time may engage in activities that are intended to bring about some learning on the part of the children. This is to say nothing more than that teaching can be done by people other than professional teachers. But what seems to characterize professional teachers is the centrality of the intention to bring about learning. The other activities that such teachers engage in are done primarily to supplement or facilitate the teaching activities. Teachers may engage in activities designed to stop unseemly or destructive behavior, to determine progress, to provide relief from tension and stress, or to achieve many other ends. These all can be related to the general intention of teaching. These kinds of activities are seen as providing a basis or an environment in which learning can be promoted. Other professionals who may engage in teaching activities from time to time would use such activities as supplements to the general intention which their activity serves. A physician who teaches a patient how to perform a certain task, say to teach a diabetic how to inject insulin, does so only to further the general intention of promoting the patient's health. So, in professional teaching, the general intention of teaching is the central intention of the activity.

The central intention of an activity, I want to claim, defines the activity for all of those in the situation; in other words, it creates what I will call an "intentional situation." A teacher cannot exist in isolation; the activity of teaching requires a student or students. One cannot try to bring about learning unless there is someone to benefit, or possibly benefit, from the activity. It is the intention of the teacher that gives meaning to the situation for the students. When teaching takes place students find themselves in situations where someone else is engaging in activities designed to make them learn something. They are expected to submit themselves to the situation; the situation becomes for them one in which the teacher's intention sets the framework for their activity. They find that a wide range of activities and conditions becomes expected of them. Their intentions can be quite irrelevant in deciding the nature of their experience in the classroom. The teacher determines the nature of their experience. The decisions a teacher makes about what is to be learned set the situation for the students.

An activity is a teaching activity because of the intention under which it is carried out. To understand that an activity is a teaching activity, then, requires one to understand the beliefs and intentions of the actor.

For students to see that what the teacher is doing is actually teaching requires the students to see the teacher's intention and beliefs. Students can only understand what is going on about them in the classroom by understanding the teacher's intentions. Thus, again, it is the intention of the teacher that defines the situation for all those involved in it. A teacher wants the students in a class to learn something: the causes of the French Revolution, to recognize a certain sound, to perform a skill of gymnastics. The students come to the class for a variety of reasons: they may be compelled by law or social norms to be there, they may have an interest in learning the topic, or they may have an end in view for which the class serves as a means. Typically their intention will not be to learn the causes of the French Revolution, to recognize the particular sound or to perform the particular gymnastics' skill. Regardless of their reasons for being in the classroom, the teacher's intention for them to learn one of these particular items defines the situation for them in the classroom. They submit, as it were, to the teacher's intention, and the knowledge or skill to be learned becomes the focus of their attention. Understanding what the teacher intends enables them to understand the situation in which they find themselves. This understanding makes sense of the classroom experience for them. The teacher's intention becomes the student's intention. It is this sharing of intentions that creates an intentional situation out of the intentional activity of the teacher. When the context becomes an intentional situation, it allows the activity of teaching to proceed.

One of the most striking features of classrooms is the fact that students come to accept the discipline of the teacher and the subject. Whether it is a group of children in an elementary classroom wrestling with the mysteries of multiplication or a group of undergraduates in a university lecture hall wrestling with the mysteries of Plato, in both cases, the students engage in activities that are defined by the teacher's intention. In order to make sense of the particular situation, they must come to understand the intention of the teacher; they must come to participate in the intentional situation that the teacher's intention has created. To a large extent they do. Students, regardless of the intentions, if any, they might have brought to the class, soon become active, even willing, participants in the activities of the classroom. Much of the writing on teaching deals with the question of how to engage students in the learning activities of the classroom. My point is more fundamental: that they become involved is a necessary condition for teaching to proceed and this involvement requires understanding on the student's part. This is, of course, not to deny the importance of teachers taking steps to engage students in learning even though teaching may even be successful if the teacher takes no such steps. A teacher can say to students, "You are going to learn this whether you want to or not," and proceed to get them to learn. Such a statement, in spite of its lack of pedagogical soundness, may be sufficient to create the intentional situation which allows students to share the intention with the teacher.

If, however, students cannot understand the intention of the teacher so that they cannot make sense of the situation in which they find themselves, the teaching is bound to be unsuccessful. If the teacher's intentions and beliefs remain hidden, the students will not be able to determine the meaning of the situation or, in other words, the situation will make no sense to them. If they do not see the teacher as a teacher, that is as one who intends for others to learn, they will not see themselves as students and so will have no reason to engage in any activity that might involve their learning something. Such cases are hard to imagine or describe because we typically do not see others as engaging in purposeless behavior. When faced with someone engaged in an activity, no matter how mysterious, we attribute to them some intention. If their intention is not clear to us we may have to formulate some possible intention under which we can view the other's activity. In classroom contexts, the student's experience may be such that no matter how opaque the teacher's intention, it is reasonable to infer that the teacher is trying to teach something. In such a case, the student may take on the role of student without being at all clear what is expected.

The intentional situation of teaching is based on the teacher's intention to bring about some particular learning. In order for students to participate meaningfully with the teacher in the activities designed to bring about this learning, they must participate in the intentional situation with the teacher. They do this by coming to understand the beliefs and intentions of the teacher. Once students have made a judgment concerning what the teacher is about, they can enter into the situation and participate in the teacher/student relation. Experience tells us that making these judgments is not difficult for students. People at all levels and abilities are able to see what is intended for them by teachers, and so they are able to become students in their classrooms. The statements of teachers and the contexts in which they act all contribute to revealing to students the nature of the activities they are to engage in. Young children go to school for a variety of reasons ranging from the sheer enjoyment of it to compulsion and coercion by their parents. They rarely go, I would submit, with the avowed intention of wanting to learn multiplication tables. Teachers who intend for students to learn the multiplication table are able, with little effort, to engage students in intentional teaching situations where the activities of students and teacher are focused around the multiplication table. That is, the intention of the teacher defines the situation for the students and enables them to participate in learning. If they never came to see the teacher's intention, they would not be able to participate in the teaching situation. The obvious and startling fact, to me, is that students do come to see the teacher's intention on a regular and routine basis.

That these judgments are made with ease by students at all levels does not mean that that these judgments are necessarily unproblematic. There are several ways in which the teacher's intentions and actions can frustrate students in their efforts to understand the teacher's beliefs and actions and, hence, in their efforts to participate in the intentional situation. Although the actions of the teacher can frustrate the students, they need not defeat them.[4]

One difficulty that students can face in making sense of the teaching situation stems from what I shall call a teacher's ignorance. If the actions a teacher performs to bring about his or her intention are such that as a matter of fact they are not likely to realize the intention, then such a case is one of ignorance. The teacher is mistaken in the belief that the actions will realize the intention. Here students will still be able to participate in an intentional situation; but because the actions of the teacher are not those that would, as a matter of fact, bring about the teacher's intention, the students will be participating in a situation whose point is other than that intended by the teacher. The story goes that a number of years ago, a nondirective method of teaching the principles of the equal arm balance was developed. Brightly colored equal arm balances were constructed out of plastic. Pairs of children were given these balances to play with; no instructions were given. After time, almost all of the children discovered the principle of the equal arm balance; they found that the products of the mass of the weights and the distance of the weights from the fulcrum were equal when it was in balance. But one pair of children never discovered this. For them the concern was to get the right colored objects together so that the appearance of this strange contraption was aesthetically pleasing. For them it was an art lesson, not a science lesson. Here, the teacher's intention was for students to learn the principles of the equal arm balance. The teacher was, however, mistaken in believing that the action performed to carry out this intention would reveal the intention; the action, it turned out, was consistent with a quite different intention. The two students who saw the exercise as one in art were able to make sense of the situation; they saw it as a situation in which their ideas on the relations of color could be tested. Indeed, since the teacher provided the means for testing colors, they could see it as a teaching situation. But, these students interpreted the situation differently than the teacher intended. Here, the teacher's mistaken belief that the actions would reveal the intended learning frustrated the particular teaching in this case, but it did not prevent the students from entering into an intentional situation with the teacher. One can surmise from such a case that an attentive teacher would realize the mistake and would adapt the teaching so as to prevent future misinterpretations. The ignorance can be overcome.

A more difficult case, and one hopes a rarer case, is irrationality on the part of the teacher. Here, it is not only the case that the teacher is mistaken in believing that the actions will realize the intention, it is also the case that the teacher cannot or will not come to see the mistake when it is pointed out.[5] Here, a teacher might hold a particular view in spite of all evidence to the contrary and may be unwilling or unable to see that the contrary evidence defeats the view. In such a case, the teacher who intends to teach the view is acting irrationally. To describe such a case would require a lengthy diversion. To sketch a case we need only to imagine a case where a teacher holds some bizarre view such as the teaching of astrology as fact and where the teacher is able to provide rationalizations to counter all the standard criticisms of astrology. Here, the teacher is acting irrationally because the view is held in spite of reasonable and compelling evidence to the contrary. What are students to make of such a situation? If the students are to participate in the intentional situation with the teacher, they will have to make sense of the situation. To make sense of the situation, they have to understand the teacher's intentions and beliefs. To do this they will have to see the teacher's actions as being efficacious in bringing about the intention. This amounts to crediting the teacher with being rational. If they do not see that the intention they credit to the teacher is consistent and related to the teacher's actions, they cannot see what the teacher is doing as making sense and, so, cannot participate in the intentional situation. So, if they are to be students in a teacher/student relationship, they must see the teacher as being rational. This means that even an irrational teacher does not prevent the establishment of an intentional situation in which students participate. This has an important pedagogical implication. The logic of the teaching situation makes the work of the irrational teacher much easier. Because the students must credit the teacher with acting rationally in order for them to be students in the intentional situation, the irrational teacher is seen by students as being rational. This enables the irrational teacher to teach the bizarre material to students who, if the teacher is competent, will not realize that it is bizarre. There are two lessons here. One is that even irrationality on the part of the teacher does not prevent students from entering intentional situations with teachers. The second is that undesirable teaching is not prevented by this account of teaching which sees it as depending on the creation of such intentional situations.

A final way in which the creation of intentional situations is problematic is the case of unconscious intentions. A teacher may have a particular intention for students to learn something and a set of beliefs how to bring about this learning. But the teacher may also have unconscious intentions that determine the beliefs. That is, the actions that a teacher carries out may be a result of unconscious intention rather than the avowed intention. A teacher may state that his intention is to teach students to think for themselves, but in his examination procedures he penalizes students who disagree with him even when they have grounds for doing so. In such a case, we might say that his real intention is different from his avowed intention and that, since he is unwilling or unable to state his real intention, it is at this point an unconscious intention. Students facing such a teacher will have to attempt to make sense of the situation in which they find themselves. The teacher's avowed intention and his actions may be at such variance that students cannot make sense of the situation and cannot enter into the intentional situation. This is the extreme case. A more likely occurrence is for students to infer the teacher's real intention from his actions and to disregard the avowed intention. I once took a university course which dealt with Brazil. The instructor once said that in the course we would learn to speak Portuguese. When Portuguese was never heard or seen in the course we simply dismissed the teacher's stated intention and got on with what he was actually teaching. Students with experience in dealing with intentional situations perhaps will be able to discern the real intention governing the activity at hand. One cannot help but think that teaching situations where the teacher's avowed intention is the real intention will be more successful. Students who do not have to spend time determining what the point of the teaching is will have more time to spend learning what is being taught. But the basic point here is that even teachers who act from unconscious intentions do not necessarily prevent the establishment of intentional situations. At the extreme, though, where the teacher's avowed intention is so at odds with the teaching actions, students may not be able to make sense of what the teacher is about and so may not be able to participate in the intentional situation of being a student.

Being a student

I have argued that teaching is an activity in which one person has the intention to bring about some learning in another person. The intention of the teacher creates a situation, an intentional situation, which gives significance not only to the teacher but to others in that situation, the students. I now want to explore in more detail what it means to be a student.[6]

Our first expectation would be that the counterpart of teaching is learning. This, it turns out, is misleading. Learning is quite independent of teaching. First, learning can occur outside the teaching situation. Much learning, if not most, takes place without a teacher. A person can learn on one's own, from experience, and in situations that are not teaching situations. Learning one's native tongue, surely one of the great intellectual achievements of a person's life, is not something typically done in teaching situations. Rather, it seems that a more adequate description of this learning is that the children "pick up" language through their experience and their interactions with parents and other speakers of the language. Children learn much about judging intentions, moods and feelings of others through games, conversations with others and the daily events of life. Much information about the world is learned through independent reading, television and other media, and conversations. None of these contexts is appropriately described as a teaching situation, but they are all contexts in which learning can and does occur.

As well, learning need not occur in teaching situations. Teaching is an activity that attempts to bring about learning; it is not an activity that necessarily results in learning. Teaching need not be identified with successful teaching. The basic notion of teaching under consideration here is that it intends to achieve learning; but, as is the case with all intentions, it can be subverted, futile or misplaced. That one intends to teach does not guarantee that one will be successful at it. This means that learning is not the necessary outcome of acts of teaching. This is, of course, in accord with common sense and usage. We all know of cases, and may even have been participants in them, in which learning did not result from teaching. So, in this way as well, teaching and learning are not necessarily connected.

Finally teaching and learning can function in quite different ways, which further suggests that they are independent. As has already been discussed, teaching is clearly an intentional activity. Learning is not always an intentional activity; it can also describe the outcome of an activity. When we say that someone is engaged in learning something, we can be saying that the person is engaged in an activity that may result in learning. Viewing a classroom and saying of the children that they are learning multiplication does not report what is being observed. We do not see children learning, we see them practicing set examples, listening to a teacher, working on a problem or engaged in some other activity. Nor must such a report be, and here is the central difference from teaching, a report of what the children intend to be doing. Children can learn multiplication in spite of their purposes at the time. Learning multiplication is something that can happen to one as a result of engaging in certain other activities, and one can learn multiplication without having the intention to do so. When an activity has a particular outcome, we can say that learning has occurred. When an activity has learning as its outcome in some typical or general way, we may call the activity a learning activity. Unlike teaching, where the activity is determined by the intention of the agent, these learning activities are not characterized by the intentions of the agent. They are, rather, descriptions of the activity that refer to the results, or typical results, of the activity. In the same way that some activities can be boring, frustrating or exhilarating, without anyone intending them to be, some activities can be learning activities. Further, learning can be the unintended and unexpected outcome of activities. Going to the movies can result in learning that the price of popcorn has gone up again. Going to school can result in children learning certain mores, say the value of punctuality, of their society.

Because, then, of these differences between how the concepts of teaching and learning function, they are quite different notions. It is thus misleading to identify the counterpart of the teacher as a learner.

The parallel activity of being a teacher in an intentional situation is being a student. Since we have no word to use here, I will refer to this as "studenting."[7] As I have suggested, "studenting" is not the same thing as learning. It is not, as well, the same as being a student in a classroom. A person can be identified as a student in a classroom without engaging in "studenting." One can attend school without engaging in the activities of the school or participating in the intentional situation of teaching. Such students are an interesting type of school dropout. They still attend school but not in the capacity of student that I want to explain. Let me turn now to the positive sense of this odd term that I have introduced.

To be a student is, as I have already suggested, to be a participant in an intentional situation with a teacher. It is the teacher's intention that creates the situation; the intention that someone learn something establishes the relation between teacher and student. The activity of teaching requires necessarily that there be students. These people must see themselves, in some sense, as students for the relation to exist. What does it mean to see oneself as a student? To be a student requires that the person have the intention to learn. It is not necessary that the person come to the situation with the intention to learn something, but once in the situation the person needs to act in accord with this intention. A child coming to school need not have the intention to learn, say, the multiplication table, but a child may find himself in a context where the teacher has the intention for him to learn the multiplication table. Although the child is attending the class, he need not be "studenting" yet. Once the child submits himself to the teacher's intention and makes it his own, he becomes a student. When the child agrees, as it were, to make a stab at learning the multiplication table, the child enters into the teaching relation with the teacher and becomes a student. The teacher's intention defines the teaching situation; when others take on this intention as their own, they enter the relation and become students. The first difference, then, between students and others who might find themselves in contact with teachers is that students have taken on the teacher's intention as governing their action in the situation. To teach multiplication to children requires that the children come to see multiplication as something to be learned. They, for whatever reason, see the task or material to be learned as impinging on themselves or as relevant to them in some way. The teacher's decision about what is important to be learned has been conveyed to them so that they, too, see it as important to learn the material. The teacher's intention has become intersubjective when the others become students.

The teacher's intention, then, defines the situation for the students, and the teacher's intention becomes the students' intention in the situation in that it governs their activity as students. Students, to be students, must see the teacher as engaging in purposive behavior. The actions the teacher performs in the context of teaching will be seen by the students as being related to a particular end. If this is not the case, the students can make no sense of what the teacher is about and so cannot see themselves as students. Students must credit the teacher with a minimum of rationality in that the teacher must be seen as acting in ways in which the actions performed are connected with the end to be achieved. As indicated earlier, the teacher's actions may be frustrated, or at least made less clear, by his or her ignorance, irrationality or unconscious intentions. When these factors intervene, the students must try to make sense of what the teacher is doing in order to remain as students. If no sense can be made of what the teacher is doing, then, of course, the students will cease to be students, they become dropouts of a sort. They will remain present in the classroom, they may even go through the motions of being a student: listening to the teacher, responding to questions, completing problem sets, writing examinations. But if they can see no purpose or intention that governs the activity, what is going on about them will make no sense.

What is most likely to occur, though, is that in the absence of something from the teacher that reveals the nature of the intentional situation, the students will determine, on their own and in their own way, what sense is to be attributed to the teacher's activity. The situation can be a meaningful one only if the teacher's activity is related to an end. If this is not clear to students, due to ignorance, irrationality or unconscious intentions on the part of the teacher, students will have to attribute some intention to the teacher. The alternative is for the situation to remain meaningless for the students. So, the presumption of rationality in teaching situations leads students to make sense of their situation in any way that they can. Clearly, clarity on the part of the teacher will help the students to see the situation in the same way as the teacher. It can prevent students and teachers from seeing the same situation in different ways and from acting at cross purposes. But students can be misled. In the extreme case of a teacher whose beliefs about the material to be taught are irrational, the students will presume that the teacher is acting in a rational way, that the teacher's actions are related to an intention. The students can be led into believing that an irrational situation is rational.

This point can be seen in another way: in terms of a relation of trust between the teacher and student. When a person enters into the relation of being a student to someone else, the student must have some degree of trust in the other person. If one had no trust whatsoever in the other person, one simply could not be a student of that person. The degree of trust or confidence that is required here seems minimal. One does not need confidence that the other is an effective teacher, is a recognized authority on a particular topic, or is a caring and responsive teacher, however desirable these characteristics are. It seems necessary, though, that one trust the teacher to be rational, or at least to make sense, and to be more likely correct than incorrect in what one says in order for one to regard the other as a teacher. If one does not have confidence in the rationality or minimal knowledge level of another person, one could not enter into a teacher/student relation with the other person. We all, I think, have experience of dealing with others of whom we lack confidence in their ability in a certain area. In such cases we, or at least I, disregard their attempts to get us to learn something. One does not enter into a teaching relation with a friend who has never played the violin because one does not have confidence in the other's ability to teach. As well, it is the case that one cannot be a student to an expert violinist if for some reason one has determined that one should not place confidence in the violinist. The trust or confidence necessary for teaching may be a presumed trust. Young children, for example, trust their teachers, not because the teacher has provided specific grounds for that trust, but because the children are in a context where it is presumed that the teacher is worthy of trust. Children can become students because they trust the teacher in general. Again, of course the trust can be betrayed. Children may have trust in teachers who in fact should not be trusted. The point here is only that some trust or confidence is necessary. One cannot be a student to a teacher if one has a total lack of confidence in the teacher's ability to realize the intention of teaching.

This sense of trust which is implicit in the teaching relationship can be clarified and illuminated by comparing it with an influential account of trust.[8] Annette Baier's discussion of trust is intended to show its importance to moral philosophy and to explain its relative absence from discussions in that field. Trust is important to moral philosophy because, "it seems fairly obvious that any form of cooperative activity, including the division of labor, requires the cooperators to trust one another to do their bit."[9] As teaching is an activity which involves students, it, too, is a cooperative activity and hence requires trust between teachers and students. Baier offers the following as an analysis of trust: "Trust, then, on this first approximation, is accepted vulnerability to another's possible but not expected ill will (or lack of good will) toward one."[10] To trust another is to put oneself in a position where one is open to the ill will of another but where one expects that ill will not to be exercised. I trust my physician because I know that he could provide a medication for my ailment that could cause me great discomfort and could even kill me, but I expect him not to exercise this ill will towards me. In this way, I am vulnerable to his ill will but in trusting him I expect him not to show this ill will. This analysis of trust has clear applications in many cases of teaching. To choose an extreme, but clear, example, consider a person deciding to learn mountain climbing from an instructor. Here, the student would recognize her vulnerability to the possible ill will of the teacher but in deciding to go ahead with the lessons she expects the teacher not to act in ways that would show ill will; in short the student trusts the teacher. In other cases involving teaching, the application of this analysis is less clear. The student enrolling in a university would see the possibility of ill will on the part of his teachers, but in not expecting that ill will to be shown, he trusts his university instructors. In such a case, what is being entrusted to the teacher is quite broad, and so greater discretion is given to the teacher over what will count as fulfilling the trust. In the case of learning how to mountain climb, the person trusts the teacher to provide instruction in a narrow range of skills, and so if the trust is betrayed, it would be done so in quite clear and precise ways. When we entrust our university education to a set of teachers, we are giving them wide discretion over what they might do. In this way, university teachers are like, to use Baier's examples,[11] surgeons and plumbers: we trust them to act on our behalf, but just what they do to educate us we must leave to them. When students are individuals making voluntary choices about their education this analysis of trust is applicable. As Baier states, these are dimensions of trust "which show up most clearly in trust between articulate adults, in a position to judge one another's performance, and having some control over their degree of vulnerability to others."[12] But, of course, these dimensions are just what do not hold in many cases of teaching.

A greater challenge to this position is seen if we focus on students who are not articulate and who do not have control over their vulnerability to others. Young children who attend school as a result of compulsory education laws would be obvious examples of such students. It is my contention that for teaching to take place with such students a degree of trust is required. From what I have said of Baier's position, it is not at all clear that her analysis of trust would be relevant in such cases. To stop here would be most unfair to Baier; her clear emphasis is on trust in dependent relationships. She extends her discussion to an infant's trust in her parents. Such an extension would clearly cover the case of the young child in school. If we can understand how an infant would trust her parents, we can understand how a young child can trust his teacher.

Baier's account of infant trust[13] is to point out that infants are in a relation of total dependence on their parents. Such dependence need not result in the infant trusting the parent, but if the infant is to survive, some trust must exist—"enough to accept offered nourishment, enough not to attempt to prevent such close approach."[14] Baier suggests that such trust may be innate and provides the possibility or basis for the existence of other forms of trust. As well, infant trust need not be won. Since mere survival depends on it, it must exist as a *sine qua non* of life. It is not something that can be established or reasoned about prior to adoption.

The form of trust that exists in the teaching situation is similar to infant trust. It is a *sine qua non* of teaching in that in its absence teaching would be a futile exercise. The absence of trust in the teaching situation would be indicated by cynicism, extreme skepticism, or total inattention on the part of the student. If the student ignored or disbelieved anything the teacher might say or do, there would be no possibility of teaching. Young children in schools do not, of course, decide to trust their teachers, but neither are they cynics or skeptics. Rather, they trust teachers to provide them with something in much the same way that they trust their parents. As students become older and learn about different forms of trust, they will come to trust others, including their teachers, in ways that come closer to the analysis given above. They will eventually become like the mountain-climbing student who has a clear picture of what she is entrusting to her teacher. However, one supposes that should the trust relation with a teacher be betrayed at some point in a person's education, the possibility of further trust becomes problematic. "Trust is much easier to maintain than it is to get started and is never hard to destroy."[15]

The first characteristic, then, of being a student is that to be a student one must submit to, or take on, the teacher's intention as providing meaning to the situation; the student must trust the teacher. A second characteristic is that what is being learned exerts a kind of control over the student. The person, to be a student, not only submits to the intention of the teacher; what is being taught also determines in part the actions of the person. To be a student requires that the rules that govern the material being learned also govern the student. The nature of what is being studied enters the intentional situation by influencing the activities that take place and determining what is to be a correct or appropriate activity in the context. Consider the case of learning how to multiply. The teacher's intention that students learn this creates the intentional situation. Once the members of the class come to see this intention, they can participate in it as students. The intention, that is, to learn how to multiply becomes their intention. Once they participate in the situation as students, the discipline of mathematics or, in this case, simply the rules of multiplication, govern their activity as well. What counts as appropriate behavior in this situation is determined in large part by the nature of the activity the students are engaged in; clearly the teacher's intention is not sufficient to determine what should take place in the teaching. Simply to want children to learn how to multiply does not suggest or require any particular actions to be performed. But once the decision has been made to teach multiplication, this branch of mathematics tells us much about how to proceed. Mathematics requires that certain activities, such as guessing or estimating, not be done when one is engaged in multiplication. Calculating is the only activity that is allowed here, and it is the material being taught that demands this. The teacher's intention is not sufficient to require this; the choice of material to be learned itself focuses the activities in which the teacher and students are engaged. The subject matter, however, does not entirely determine the activities in which the teacher is engaged while teaching; the teacher's professional knowledge of mathematics instruction plays a central and crucial role in determining the activities in which one engages while teaching or being a student. This topic will be the focus of my discussion later; at this point I want only to establish that being a student is not only a function of the teacher's intention, it is in part a function of the subject matter being taught.

The material to be taught in a teaching situation also influences what it means to be a student by providing the criteria for achievement or accomplishment in the teaching situation. Success in a teaching situation, at least in one sense of success, occurs when the students have learned the material being taught. What counts as learning the material is determined by the subject. It is our knowledge of mathematics that gives us the criteria for determining if a student knows how to multiply numbers correctly. The teacher does not establish criteria for success in mathematics; these are givens supplied by the subject area. We do not decide ourselves what it means for a child to be able to multiply numbers correctly. That the child gets the answers that are correct according to the rules of mathematics shows that the child can perform multiplication successfully. The same point holds in other subject areas, I believe, but less clearly. It is the practice of golf that provides the criteria for an adequate stance; literary criticism tells us what is to count as a successful interpretation of a poem. To have the intention to teach children how to stand while swinging a golf club or how to interpret a poem does not provide the critera for determining whether the student has been successful. These critera are implicit in the subject matter being taught. What counts as success or accomplishment in teaching, then, is a part of the subject matter. But the critera for success also determine, in part, the nature of the activity. So, again, the subject matter also shapes the activities that are part of the teaching situation.

Teaching and learning

Much reference has been made to the idea of learning; it is now time to focus more clearly on its relation to teaching. That there is a relation is, I hope, obvious; the nature of this relation is not at all clear. What I have said so far says that learning is related to teaching in that any understanding of teaching must see it as trying to bring about learning. Although a reference to learning occurs in any characterization of teaching, teaching and learning are not related logically. By "logical relation"

I mean a relation of implication or, in other words, of necessity or sufficiency. Teaching is neither a necessary nor a sufficient condition for learning. Teaching is not a necessary condition for learning because learning can take place without teaching. Any instance of a person learning on his or her own, without a teacher, shows that teaching is not necessary for learning to take place. Such instances are, of course, extremely common. Teaching is not a sufficient condition for learning because teaching does not imply learning. It can be true that a person is engaged in teaching something to a group of students without it being true that the students learn what is being taught to them. So teaching can occur without learning taking place.

This shows that teaching is neither necessary nor sufficient for learning, or that, in other words, there is no logical relation between teaching and learning in the most common way of understanding the notion of a logical relation. One does feel uncomfortable with this conclusion; teaching and learning are so intimately connected one feels that the relation must be logical, which is the strongest relation that can obtain between concepts. I feel that this sense of unease stems from the fact that although teaching does not imply learning, it does imply the intention to bring about learning. This is, of course, a restatement of what I have presented throughout as the root notion behind our concept of teaching. Surely one criterion for success in human activities is that one's intentions for performing the activity have been realized. If one runs a race with the intention of winning, one is successful if one does in fact win the race. If one teaches and the students do in fact learn what is being taught, then one is successful in one's teaching.[16] So, in this case, successful teaching means that the intention of the teacher to bring about learning has been fulfilled. In this way successful teaching does imply that learning has taken place. We can capture this idea, I think, by describing learning as the appropriate or desirable outcome of teaching. But the fact that there is a logical relation between successful teaching and learning does not allow us to conclude that there is a logical relation between teaching and learning.[17]

Another way of trying to identify the relation between teaching and learning is to say that the two notions are ontologically dependent.[18] A concept is ontologically dependent on another if the first concept is meaningless in the absence of the second concept. Fenstermacher introduces this notion of ontological dependence in the following way. After noting that instances of teaching do not necessarily imply instances of learning (the point made above), he says;

> But suppose R [a student] never learns C [the material being taught] as a result of his association with P [a teacher]. Can it still be maintained that P is teaching R? Yes. Take an analogous set of concepts, racing and winning. I can race until the end of time, never win, and yet still be racing. And though

I need never win in order to race, the concept of racing would be meaningless in the absence of any concept of winning. That is, if *no one ever* won, then whatever it is that people do on a track, it would not be called racing. There is a special semantic relationship between the terms 'racing' and 'winning,' such that the meaning of the former is, in many ways, dependent on the existence of the latter concept. I call this relationship ontological dependence. The notion of ontological dependence helps to explain why most of us perceive such a tight connection between teaching and learning. If no one ever learned, it is hard to imagine that we would possess the concept of teaching. For, if learning simply never occurred, what point would there be in teaching? The connection between the two concepts is tightly woven into the fabric of our language.[19]

This is the discussion of ontological dependence that is given to us; it is not sufficient for me to understand it completely, but it does seem to me to be incorrect in this case. Let me try to explain. The first point stems from the fact that the relation of ontological dependence between teaching and learning is presented by an analogy. I would submit that the relation between racing and winning is not analogous to that between teaching and learning. As I have already shown teaching is neither a necessary nor sufficient condition for learning. But running a race is a necessary, although not a sufficient, condition for winning a race.[20] The reason that the concept of racing would be meaningless without a concept of winning may be that running a race is a logically necessary condition for winning a race. The concept of racing depends on the concept of winning in that winning logically implies racing so that without a concept of winning there could be no concept of racing. Here, we have only to appeal to the more usual notion of logical necessity to make the point; we do not have to create a concept of ontological dependence to make the point.

But this does not show that ontological dependence is not the relation between teaching and learning. The point was made by analogy. Even if the analogy breaks down and we can dispense with the notion of ontological dependence in the case of racing and winning, it may still be the case that the relation holds between teaching and learning. To test this claim, we must ask if it is the case that the concept of teaching would be meaningless without a concept of learning. This question can be recast into the language of necessary conditions. This question asks if the claim that there is a concept of learning is a necessary condition for the claim that the concept of teaching is meaningful. This, it should be noted, is a different relation than the one rejected earlier. There I showed that the claim that some learning has occurred is not a necessary condition for the claim that some teaching has occurred. It is the case that the fact that teaching has taken place does not imply that learning has taken place. But the question, now, is whether the fact that the concept of teaching is meaningful implies that there is a concept of learning. To put the question in this form shows, I think, that the answer to the question is obviously "yes," but it also shows that the relation is one of simple implication without the need to appeal to ontological dependence. Since, as I have argued, a part of the meaning of teaching is the intent to bring about learning, the meaningfulness of the concept of teaching implies the existence of the concept of learning, because one could not have the intent to bring about learning if there were no such thing as learning. This is to say nothing more than that teaching involves the intention to bring about learning.

The reason Fenstermacher introduces the notion of ontological dependence is to argue against the view that the relation between teaching and learning is a causal relation. "It is easy to mistake ontologically dependent relationships for causal relationships. Because the concept of teaching is dependent on a concept of learning, and because learning so often occurs after teaching, we may easily be lulled into thinking that one causes the other."[21] I shall return to the issue of causal relations between teaching and learning shortly, but here I want to argue that there is no inconsistency between claiming that two concepts are ontologically related in the sense that Fenstermacher identifies and their being causally related. Ontological dependence seems to be nothing more than the claim that for a concept, A, to be meaningful, another concept, B, must exist. Causal relations, unlike ontological dependence, hold between events or states of affairs. There seems to be no reason to maintain that because the meaningfulness of concept A implies the existence of concept B, we cannot ask if there are causal relations between states of affairs that involve A and states of affairs that involve B. Consider the case of treating and curing a disease which, unlike the case of racing and winning, is analogous to the teaching and learning. Treating a disease is neither a necessary nor sufficient condition for curing the disease; the treatment may not work or the person may recover spontaneously. But treating a disease is ontologically dependent on curing; since to treat a disease is to intend to bring about a cure, the existence of the concept of cure is necessary for the concept of treatment to be meaningful. This is entirely consistent with asking whether certain treatments for a disease do in fact cure the disease, i.e. whether the treatment causes recovery. Similarly, we can ask whether certain teaching events cause learning. The existence of this relation of ontological dependence between two concepts does not prevent us from asking whether instances of these concepts are causally related. The notion of ontological dependence, to summarize, was introduced to provide an alternative to the claims that teaching and learning are related logically or that they are related causally. I have shown that in the case of teaching this notion amounts to nothing more than the logical relation I elucidated earlier, that the intent to bring about learning is a necessary condition for the concept of teaching, and that this notion of ontological dependence is not inconsistent with the existence of causal relations between instances of teaching and learning. It is now time to consider the third alternative, which I believe is the correct one.

Thomas Green is one who claims that there is no causal relation between teaching and learning. "Teaching cannot be understood as the kind of activity that *causes* learning, because it can occur when learning does not. Moreover, learning can occur when there is no teaching."[22] The premises in this argument are, of course, true; it would be foolish to deny them. The problem is that they do not support the conclusion. The argument does not work because it appeals to an overly simple view of causation. I want to establish this point in two ways.

The first problem here is to suppose that causal statements are universally true. Some may be, but there are true causal statements that are not universal. In discussing his discomfort in claiming that teaching and learning are not causally related Green says, "Secretly, or implicitly, when we think about learning how to teach, we think of teaching, in all its aspects, as an activity directed at 'making something happen,' and the language of 'making something happen' is essentially the language of cause and effect. It has been a fundamental search of philosophers to find just that method of teaching or that system of pedagogy which will assure success, i.e. achievement. And this disposes us, whether we admit it or not, to think of teaching as the effort which produces, or results in, learning."[23] This passage takes for granted that a causal statement must provide a formula or recipe that assures the occurrence of the effect. If we could use causal language meaningfully in contexts where it is possible for the cause to occur but for the effect not to occur, Green's connection of causal language and the necessity of the effect, as is made in the above statement, would be a mistaken connection. I would submit that causal language is appropriate in such circumstances. There is no doubt that arsenic is a poison, that it causes death, but it is not inconceivable for a person to ingest arsenic without dying. The dose may be too small, the person may have developed a tolerance to lethal doses, another event may intervene to prevent the arsenic from causing harm to the person. The American Surgeon General has assured us that smoking causes cancer; but there are many smokers who live to ripe ages without developing cancer. Here we have plausible cases of causal language where the effect is not assured by the occurrence of the cause.

The kinds of causal relations that exist cover a wide ground. There are "necessary causes, sufficient causes, necessary and sufficient causes, combinations of causal factors, counteracting causes, a plurality of alternative causes, causal overdetermination, and so on."[24] What Green has shown in the passage cited above is that teaching is not, in general, a sufficient cause of learning. It is the case that not all cases of teaching are followed by, to put it in crude Humean language, cases of learning or that not all cases of teaching produce, bring about or assure cases of learning. The mistake here is to conclude from the fact that teaching is not, in general, a sufficient cause of learning that there is no causal relation between teaching and learning. Sufficient causes are only one type of causal relation; his argument does not preclude that teaching and learning are causally related in another way. I want to argue that teaching can be a causal factor in learning.[25]

To do this I will provide a framework for understanding partial causes and suggest that it is at least plausible for a case of teaching to be construed in this framework as a partial cause of a case of learning. In doing so there will be many issues that are ignored or treated superficially. The two most obvious issues to receive this treatment will be the nature of causation and the actual establishment of teaching as a causal factor of learning. That is, I will not try to provide a complete or even adequate account of causal relations; nor will I produce the evidence which shows that teaching is a causal factor in cases of learning. I feel justified, if not comfortable, in establishing a much weaker point: that teaching can be a causal factor in learning. For the position that I am developing only this is necessary. To provide a complete account of causal relations and to prove that cases of teaching are indeed causal factors in cases of learning would take me too far afield.

The framework I want to introduce is the so-called "inus" condition.[26] Consider some event or phenomenon, P. That event may be the result of a conjunction of a certain set of events or conditions, say ABC, such that whenever ABC occurs P will occur. In this case ABC is a sufficient condition for P where "sufficient condition" is to be understood as "X is a sufficient condition for Y" means that whenever an event of type X occurs, so does one of type Y. To illustrate, suppose that P is the phenomenon of death and that A is ingesting a large dose of arsenic, B is the absence of an antidote and C is that there is no tolerance to arsenic. Suppose further that research or experience tells us that whenever ABC are conjoined in this way P occurs, but that if A, B or C occurs alone P will not occur. ABC is, then, a sufficient condition for P, but each of A, B and C is insufficient for P. Suppose further that research or experience tells us that we must have each of A, B, and C for P to occur. That is, if AB, AC or BC occur, P will not occur. We can capture this by saying each of A, B and C is non-redundant, or that each must be present for P to occur. Suppose further that there are other sets of conditions or events that are sufficient for P; there are, after all, such things as cyanide and heart attacks that, with attendant conditions, cause death. For the sake of argument, let us say that all the other sets of conditions that are sufficient for P can be captured by DGH and JKL. This gives us the formula "All (ABC or DGH or JKL) are followed by P." In this formula each of ABC, DGH and JKL are sufficient for P but none of them is necessary. That is, if ABC, DGH or JKL occur P will occur, but P can occur without ABC occurring, without DGH occurring, or without JKL occurring. This formula is applicable to situations where a particular event can be produced in a variety of ways and where each of the ways is itself a set of conditions or events all of which must obtain. This would seem to be a relatively common state of affairs. Now, in light of this formula we can express the relation between A (eating arsenic) and P (death) by saying that A is "an *insufficient* but *non-redundant* part of an *unnecessary* but *sufficient* condition"[27] for P. Taking the first letters of the italicized words, we can say that A is an inus condition for P.

It is important to note the context in which the inus condition is established. It stems from a formula which, at least in the context in which I have presented it, assumes a regularity interpretation of causality. That is, I have presented the inus condition without asking whether the formula "All (ABC or DGH or JKL) are followed by P" is an adequate rendering of a causal statement. To be sure, it probably is not, but what does seem correct to say is that if several sets of conditions exhaust the range of causes of a phenomenon P, then whenever any one of the causes of P occurs, P will occur. The formula above may not be equivalent in meaning to the claim that the causes of P are ABC, DGH and JKL; but the claim that the causes of P are ABC, DGH and JKL implies the formula. So we can reasonably call each of the inus conditions in the formula a causal factor. It seems, as well, that the details of the formula do not need to be known in order to apply the notion of inus conditions. Before moving to the question of teaching and learning, consider this example from an unrelated field. An explosion on an airplane caused it to crash. There are, no doubt, many sets of conditions that would cause an airplane to crash; I am not sure that anyone could list them all. One of the set of conditions would include the explosion of a bomb on board. By itself a bomb explosion would not necessarily result in a crash; other conditions such as the size and location of the bomb as well as, perhaps, other conditions would have to be met. Without the bomb explosion the other conditions would not suffice to cause the crash. So, the bomb explosion is an inus condition; it is by itself insufficient, but is a non-redundant part of a set of conditions which itself is a sufficient but unnecessary condition for the crash. So, we can identify the explosion of the bomb as a causal factor in the crash. This shows that the notion of an inus condition is applicable even though the details of the formula cannot be supplied in detail. It also shows that an inus condition does not establish a certain causal factor as *the cause*. Other considerations would have to be appealed to in order to determine which inus condition or causal factor would be identified as the cause. Notions such as responsibility[28] or abnormality[29] have been appealed to as the basis for making this judgment.

I now want to suggest that it is plausible to see that the relation between teaching and learning is a causal relation where an instance of teaching is an inus condition for learning. We need, I think, to be a bit more specific; teaching and learning are such broad notions that it does not help much to talk of them *simpliciter*. Let us take as the phenomenon P a child learning how to multiply two-digit numbers. There are no doubt a fairly large number of sets of circumstances that would be sufficient to bring about this learning. Research in psychology and mathematics learning would, I should think, provide us with a range of ways in which children learn how to multiply two-digit numbers. I rather suspect, and most certainly hope, that one set of conditions that is sufficient for bringing about this learning would include teaching. Teaching children would not be by itself sufficient to bring about this learning, other conditions would have to be present. The children would have to possess certain knowledge, say knowing how to multiply single-digit numbers, and they would have to have certain abilities, capacities and attitudes. The exact set of conditions would have, again, to be determined by careful research into, this time, mathematics teaching. What would be the case is that teaching would be a non-redundant element of this set of conditions, if the child had the ability, attitude, background knowledge and whatever, she would not learn to multiply two-digit numbers without teaching. Thus, teaching how to multiply two-digit numbers can be an inus condition or causal factor in the child's learning of how to multiply two-digit numbers. This shows it is plausible to see teaching as a causal factor related to learning even though teaching is not by itself always sufficient to bring about learning and even though teaching is not necessary to bring about learning. The overly simplistic view of a causal relation between teaching and learning that I began with is now seen to be inadequate because there are more detailed and complicated causal relationships which are consistent with the apparent lack of relation between instances of teaching and learning.

The result of this complicated, but I hope not too tortuous, route is two-fold. First, it is now clear that research on teaching and learning is central to the practice of teaching. Because teaching can be construed as a causal factor in learning, researchers can conceptualize ways in which teaching as an inus condition is actually related to various instances of learning. Research programs and projects can, thus, be developed in terms of elucidating and discovering the inus conditions of learning. The second result is that the relation of teaching and learning is more clear. Not only is teaching conceptually related to learning as being an effort intended to bring about learning; it is also possible to see that teaching is factually or empirically related to learning as an inus condition. This gives us a grasp on how theoretical knowledge of teaching can be related to the practice of teaching. To that topic I will now turn.

CHAPTER 7

The practice of teaching

The account of teaching in the previous chapter is by no means a complete one. It ignores the empirical research on teaching, which comprises a massive literature; it ignores as well the practical experience gained by teachers. As a philosophical account it is incomplete; philosophers of education who have considered the activities of teaching have considered many more aspects of this concept than I have introduced. I hope, though, that what I have said is accurate and true as far as it goes; as limited as my story is, it does provide a basis for considering a theoretical account of the practice of teaching, which is my task in this chapter. To achieve this task, I will outline a conception of practice and use my account of teaching to show what important questions must be considered in the practice of teaching. I will then discuss the kinds of knowledge that we possess with respect to the practice of teaching. This knowledge will comprise, in a sense, the theory of teaching. The next issue I will tackle is the question of how this knowledge is utilized; this issue can be seen as the question, then, of how theory is translated into practice. Finally, I will conclude the chapter with some reflections on this general question of how the theory and practice of teaching are related. My concern in this chapter is to provide a way of understanding how teachers use their knowledge and beliefs in practice or, if you will, how they integrate theory into practice. What should be clear at this point is that unlike other positions considered earlier, I am placing the burden of discussion on the practice of teaching. Instead of identifying what a theory of education or teaching is and then moving to practice, I believe these issues are highlighted if we consider first the practice of teaching and then ask how theoretical knowledge is brought to bear on it.

A conception of practice

The notion of practice is not an easy one. It can mean the habitual or usual way of doing something; this sense of practice is appealed to when we talk of someone practicing a musical instrument or a skill. In such a case, one may repeat a certain action so as to make its performance habitual or routine. To be sure a teacher will often engage in practice of this sort, there are many things that need to be done repetitively in order to be mastered. This is not the sense of the practice of teaching that is at issue here. We are concerned in the practice of teaching, just as in the practice of medicine, law or architecture, with how the professional practitioner uses her knowledge to solve problems, to devise courses of action that respond to the circumstances one is in, or to make appropriate changes in a situation. To talk of professional practice is to talk of a much more elaborate activity than is found in our usual ways of doing things.

A conception of practice that might be appropriate for the practice of teaching is given by Alasdair MacIntyre in *After Virtue.*

> By a "practice" I am going to mean any coherent and complex form of socially established cooperative human activity through which goods internal to that form of activity are realized in the course of trying to achieve those standards of excellence which are appropriate to, and partially definitive of, that form of activity, with the result that human powers to achieve excellence, and human conceptions of the ends and goods involved, are systematically extended.[1]

Later he says, "A practice involves standards of excellence and obedience to rules as well as the achievement of goods."[2] I want to consider teaching as a practice by asking how it involves these three characteristics. But before embarking on this, there is one technical term in the characterization of practice that needs to be explained: "an internal good."

Internal goods are distinguished from external goods. Some goods are "externally and contingently attached to a practice by the accidents of social circumstances."[3] Other goods are internal to a practice in that they cannot be had in any way but by engaging in the practice. MacIntyre gives two reasons for calling goods internal: "we can only specify them in terms of" the practice and "they can only be identified and recognized by the experience of participating in the practice in question."[4] This distinction is not sufficiently clear as it stands, nor is it made more clear by the example in which MacIntyre embeds the distinction. In using the practice of playing chess as the context in which the distinction is introduced, MacIntyre uses prestige, status and money as external goods. That these meet his characterization of external goods is, I believe, clear. These are goods that can be achieved through the practice of playing chess, but their relation to chess is purely contingent. Under present social circumstances chess is a practice that can be rewarded with such things as prestige, status and money. Under other circumstances, the practice of chess could be exactly the same but it could lead to approbation, disgrace or, in a society that has made chess illegal, criminal penalties.

It is when MacIntyre discusses the internal goods of chess that the position becomes less clear. The internal goods of chess that he identifies are, "the achievement of a certain highly particular kind of analytical skill, strategic imagination and competitive intensity."[5] The same qualities, it seems, could be attached to other games, say checkers and bridge. So, there must be different kinds of analytic skills, strategic imagination and competitive intensity in chess than in checkers or bridge for the characterization to hold. Whether this is true is an issue about which I am not sure; as I am not a chess player I, by definition, am not able to recognize the goods internal to chess. With respect to other games with which I do have experience, it is not at all clear to me that there are different kinds of, say, competitive intensity that can be achieved in them. I take delight in trying to outwit and best opponents in a variety of games, but whether the competition in Scrabble and other games is of the same or of a different kind is not at all obvious to me. Another way of formulating the distinction between internal and external goods that avoids this kind of problem, but seems to retain the spirit of MacIntyre's point, is to call those goods that can be achieved, but which are contingent on the social circumstances in which the practice is performed, external to a practice and to call those goods that can be achieved regardless of the social circumstances in which the practice is performed internal to a practice. Money would still be an external good of chess, there are social circumstances where excellence in chess will bring monetary reward to a player but there are other circumstances where no such rewards could accrue. The achievement of analytic skill of a particular kind will be a good that is internal to chess because skill in playing chess will result in the development of such a skill no matter what the social circumstances are in which the game is played. The skill is developed simply as a result of playing chess. This leaves open the question of whether the analytic skill so achieved is the same or different as that developed in other practices. The skill is inherent or intrinsic in the practice, so it can still be regarded as an internal good.

I now want to consider whether teaching is a practice in MacIntyre's rich sense of practice. To give a complete answer is to attempt too much at this point; rather I want to now make plausible that teaching can be a practice. The full answer will be clear later; the tentative answer I give here will set the stage for the discussion of the chapter. To make it plausible that teaching is a practice I need, under MacIntyre's view, to consider three questions: Does teaching promote the achievement of internal goods? Are there standards of excellence inherent in the activity of teaching? When teaching, are there rules to which one is obedient? I will consider the questions in this order.

Given the discussion of internal goods above, I need to identify those goods, if any, that can be achieved in teaching under any set of social circumstances. There are many external goods that can be achieved through teaching. Money, status and prestige, to use MacIntyre's examples of external goods of chess, sadly are not common external goods of teaching at present. There are those who would have it that the problems of teaching and education can be solved by increasing the likelihood of achieving these goods through teaching or, at least, that by increasing the opportunity for financial reward through teaching, greater prestige and status would follow as consequences. At any rate, these goods are dependent on the social circumstances in which one finds oneself and, so, are not internal goods. Winning the respect and admiration of others are goods that can be achieved through teaching, but they are external goods as well. We all have known teachers whom we respected and admired for their ability to help us learn, for introducing us to new ways of thinking, for encouraging us to master difficult material. Some may even have been so fortunate to have had students respect and admire them on these grounds. These goods are external in that there are social circumstances where the achievement of these goods would be unachievable. A society where learning is not valued would be one in which a person could not gain the respect and admiration of others for helping others to learn. So the respect and admiration that a teacher might earn is contingent upon the values of the society in which one teaches. That this is a realistic possibility, rather than merely a conceivable one, is a more difficult question. It is difficult, if not impossible, to conceive of a society in which teaching and learning do not take place.[6] To say that teaching and learning are necessary features of human society is not to say that those who bring about learning are necessarily respected or admired. Human society may not be able to exist without learning and teaching but those who bring about such learning may not achieve respect or admiration for what they do. The learning that does take place may be seen as a necessary evil, something to be accepted begrudgingly. In such a case teachers will not be able to earn respect or admiration for their work. So, respect and admiration are external, not internal, goods of teaching.

To find an internal good of teaching, we will have to return to the characterization of teaching presented in the last chapter. Since an internal good is something achievable in the activity in any set of social circumstances, the internal goods will have to be related to what holds necessarily for the activity. What is necessary for a teaching activity is the intent to bring about learning on the part of others and the creation of the consequent intentional situation in which students take up the intention as governing their activity. The achievement that is possible in teaching activities is, of course, to bring about learning. No matter what the social circumstances that may exist this is always and necessarily a possible accomplishment. Can we say simply that the internal good of teaching is the achievement of learning in others? I want to say both yes and no. A teacher who is able to get students to learn that which is intended is one who has achieved what teaching is about. She has accomplished the good that can be met through teaching. The good that results from helping others to learn what one intends for them to learn is an internal good of teaching. This line of thought indicates that the good of teaching is simply the achievement of learning in others. One may balk at such an easy account. The basis for disagreement is that the achievement of learning may not count as a good; one wants to ask what is being learned and the means the teacher is using to bring about the learning. The specific content that one is teaching may raise questions. A teacher who intends for his students to learn how to cheat on their income taxes may achieve this, but we may be, and probably are, reluctant to say that the newly learned ability to cheat is an internal good. There are also great differences in views on the nature of what is to be learned. Some may hold that the internal good of teaching is the achievement of mastery of a certain area of knowledge or skill; others may hold that the internal good lies in helping students to learn to be independent and healthy individuals; still others may hold that it lies in helping students learn so that their forms of thinking are enhanced and broadened.[7] Finally, one wants to say that no matter what is learned, if the teacher uses immoral means to bring it about, say indoctrination, the achievement of learning cannot be an internal good. This line of thought suggests that to identify the internal good of teaching one will have to be much more specific in the formulation of the good than to say simply that it is the achievement of the intended learning.

It seems that any account of the internal good of teaching will have to take both lines of thought into consideration. If we take seriously the requirement that an internal good is something that can be achieved in any instance of the practice and is not contingent upon social circumstances, then, in looking for the internal good, we cannot go much beyond the intention to bring about learning, for that is all that is necessary to every case of teaching. The nature of the learning to be achieved and the means used to bring about learning will, to some degree, be dependent on social circumstance. In an affluent society it may be possible to afford the luxury of teaching so that students learn to be self-fulfilled individuals. In a society on the edge of extinction, it may only be possible to teach so that students learn enough to survive. In both cases, the internal good is the achievement of learning; however, what counts as desirable learning will vary. It seems, in conclusion, that the best we can do in identifying the internal good of teaching is to leave it at the achievement of learning. What is recognized, though, is that there will be much variation in what is regarded as the appropriate learning for individuals.

A second feature of practices in this conception is that practices involve standards of excellence. Does teaching fit this requirement? That it does is, I think, clear; how it does is far less clear. The internal good of teaching, the achievement of learning on the part of students, also provides the basis for the standards of excellence of teaching. One excels at teaching, at least in part, if one's students learn what is being taught or, a bit more precisely, if one causes students to learn what is being taught. The success a teacher meets is a matter of degree. A teaching activity may be successful with one student but not with another. Some students may learn more than others. It is the variability of success in teaching that allows us to distinguish competent, good and outstanding teachers. An excellent teacher would be one who has a high degree of success in his or her teaching. So we can clearly talk about standards of excellence with respect to teachers. We can, as well, talk about excellent teaching independent of the teacher. The basis for identifying such would seem again to lie in the ability or potential of the teaching to bring about learning. We would say of a piece of teaching that it was excellent if it seemed likely to bring about the kind of learning that is desired. So, we can apply the notion of involving standards of excellence to teaching, but to leave the point at this level misses much that is important.

To say that a piece of teaching is an example of excellent teaching is to say that it is teaching that would achieve the desired kind of learning. Where this issue becomes less clear is the specification of desired kinds of learning. Differences on this point can, of course, result in differences on the evaluation of instances of teaching. An example of teaching can be described as excellent because of its clarity, precision, logical structure and the like. Such teaching may be regarded as excellent because it is very likely to result in the students learning the information that is contained in the lesson. Alternatively, teaching that is open, unstructured and unclear in its outcomes may be described as excellent by one who feels it is important for students to learn to identify issues and deal with them in their own ways. Differences in desired learning can result, then, in differences in what will count as excellent teaching.

Teaching, then, involves standards of excellence but the standards will depend on judgments made about the kind of learning that it is appropriate or desirable for students to learn. In some practices, the standards of excellence will be relatively straightforward. In the practice of chess, the example referred to earlier, it would seem that there would be relatively less debate about the standards of excellence to be applied. Teaching is a practice that relates to many other concerns of life in ways that result in there being different and inconsistent views of what counts as a standard of excellence. It is clear, though, that teaching does involve such standards even though the difficulties and controversies in identifying the standards will be great.

A similar sort of point holds with respect to the third feature of practices; obedience to rules. That teaching involves obeying rules is clear; how the rules are to be specified is much more difficult. As an intentional activity with internal goods and standards of excellence, teaching is a rule-governed activity.[8] To say that an activity is rule-governed is to say that there are right and wrong ways to perform an action. Some moves in chess, to revert to that example, are allowed, others are not; the rules of chess determine which is which. An activity is rule-governed if it is possible to make mistakes in the performance of the activity. Teaching is an activity in which it is possible to make mistakes. In observing someone teach or in reflecting on one's own teaching it is surely possible to say that a particular move should not have been performed, that it was a mistake to have done that in this context. That this is possible is all that is needed to establish that the activity is rule-governed. When an activity has a point, as in the cases of chess and teaching, it makes sense to identify possible mistakes in the performance of the activity. The purpose of an activity establishes what would count as an appropriate achievement for the activity and, so, what one does while performing the activity can be either conducive to bringing about the achievement or not; that is, it can be appropriate or mistaken.

That it is possible to be mistaken in the performance of an activity means that it is possible to correct oneself in its performance. Indeed, correcting oneself is an indication that one is engaged in a rule-governed activity. To use the rather more straightforward chess example again, in playing chess there are two sorts of mistakes one can make, what we might call basic mistakes and strategic mistakes. A basic mistake is where one violates one of the explicit rules of chess, say, by moving the knight straight ahead. When such a mistake is pointed out, the person will correct his or her actions so that moves of the knight correspond to the rules. If the person refused to make corrections to basic mistakes, we would have to conclude that the person is not playing chess. Certainly one would not attempt to play chess with a person who saw no need to correct one's moves so that they were in accord with the rules. But, there are strategic mistakes in chess as well. In chess, as in most other activities requiring a degree of thought, there are techniques and strategies that become part of the lore of the activity, although not part of the explicit rule book. Some openings in chess are better than others even though all of them are in accord with the rules of moving chess pieces. A person can, thus, make mistakes in chess that are strategic in nature in that they are not in violation of the explicit rules but are likely to lessen the chances of success in the game. A person who refused to correct such mistakes could not be said to be playing some other game, instead such a person could be rightly accused of failing to take the game seriously. The person would be neglecting the internal good of the activity. So, some rules are constitutive of the activity itself, others are constitutive of success in the activity. To engage in the activity seriously, one must be willing to see the rules as correctives to one's moves when performing the activity. To see rules as correctives to what one does is to put oneself in the position of being obedient to the rules of the activity.

The conclusion I draw from this is that because teaching is a rule-governed activity and because rule-governed activities require that one see the rules as correctives, the activity of teaching meets this third feature of practices which is that a practice involves obedience to rules. Using my distinction between basic and strategic rules, we would have to say that the rules of teaching are largely, if not totally, strategic. There is no explicit rule book we can provide to teachers, as much as some would want one, that will tell them what to do. As I have tried to argue, it is the intention of teaching that is constitutive of the activity, not the rules of teaching. The rules of teaching that we are able to provide are strategic rules. Such rules are ones that, if followed, will contribute towards success in the activity. Success in teaching involves the achievement of learning on the part of students but, as I have said before, there are deep and abiding differences in what counts as appropriate learning. As a consequence, there are divisions in what would count as appropriate strategic rules for teaching.

Some strategies for achievement of the internal goods of teaching will be accepted by some, rejected by others. The process-product research on teaching tells us that teachers who move about their classrooms are teachers who tend to have fewer students who go "off task" and, consequently, are teachers whose students show greater achievement in the material being learned. If one accepts achievement in learning, as demonstrated on achievement tests, as the standard of appropriate learning, this research provides a strategic rule of teaching. If one sees the development of a healthy, integrated personality as the appropriate result of teaching, one probably would not see this result of research as providing much in the way of useful strategy. So, again, the specific rules that are to be obeyed when engaged in the practice of teaching are difficult to specify because such rules are strategies for achieving the standards of excellence of teaching and there is fundamental disagreement over what is to be accepted as the standards. However, the more fundamental point has been established, that teaching involves obedience to rules, even though we cannot establish a set of uncontroversial rules.

Teaching, thus, meets MacIntyre's three characteristics of practice: it has internal goods and it involves standards of excellence and obedience to rules. This establishes that, at least in this sense, teaching is a practice. But although this makes some progress, it still leaves much to do before the relation of theory and practice in teaching is to be understood. My next step along the way to that understanding is to look at what I will call "the knowledge base of teaching." This will provide us with a look at what we might call, in a misleading way, "the theory of teaching."

The knowledge base of teaching

One result of this conception of practice is that one cannot engage in a practice in ignorance, that is, one must possess some knowledge in order to participate in a practice. That a practice involves internal goods, standards of excellence and obedience to rules means that a practitioner must have some knowledge about the activity, for without any knowledge of the practice one could not identify internal goods, aim for standards of excellence or obey rules. Knowledge is often, if not always, the result of investigation, reflection, experiment or experience, which are just the sorts of things that can be seen to be theoretical. The connections, then, between theory and practice will begin to be seen when we look at the knowledge that is required for one to engage in a practice. I want to consider several areas of knowledge that are involved in teaching. I believe that some knowledge from each area is necessary for the practice of teaching, but I do not claim that there is specific knowledge in each area which is required for anyone who wishes to engage in the practice of teaching. Let me turn to these areas of knowledge which provide what I am calling the knowledge base of teaching.

Causal knowledge

In Chapter 6, I sketched a causal theory of teaching. There I claimed that one's teaching activity can be a part of a set of conditions that cause students to learn. Here, I want to elaborate on that notion by discussing the causal knowledge that teachers can employ in their efforts to bring about learning. The first point that I want to make is that some causal knowledge is necessary.

The basis for making this claim is, of course, the causal theory of teaching, which says that the relation between teaching and learning is that a teaching action can be a causal factor of learning in that of the various sets of conditions which are sufficient, but not necessary, for the learning of X, one set of conditions may contain teaching as a necessary and non-redundant element. To illustrate, a person may learn that the Battle of Waterloo was fought in 1815. In identifying the causal factors that may be responsible for this we can produce different sets of conditions that would bring about this effect; the person might have read it in a history text, it could have been a question on a television game show, it might have been taught to him. Each of these is one part of a set of conditions, that is, not only could it have been a question on a game show, but he would have had to be paying attention, have had some sort of confidence in the reliability of the question author, and so on. In the case of the person learning this fact from teaching not only would the teacher have to include it in the teaching but the students would have to be paying attention, have the appropriate background to make sense of what the teacher is doing, trust the veracity of the teacher, and so on. So, we would have a set of conditions that include the teacher's actions, which is a sufficient but not necessary condition for learning that the Battle of Waterloo took place in 1815. Which set of conditions is to be identified as the cause of the learning is, of course, an empirical question. One would have to examine the case to determine what, in fact, was the responsible agent for the learning. This causal theory does not tell us what in fact caused a particular event. It only tells us that teaching can be a causal factor in learning.

The causal theory does not say that all teaching results in learning, nor does it say that all learning is the result of teaching. It does say that it is possible to explain instances of learning by instances of teaching. Since the internal good of the practice of teaching is the achievement of the intended learning, the successful practice of teaching will be explained by locating the causal factors that brought it about. If teaching is successful, then this success can be explained by showing what teaching actions caused the learning to occur. The practice of teaching strives to realize its internal good—the achievement of learning; this is done by performing actions which cause that learning to occur. For teachers to be successful in their practice, their actions must explain, and explain causally, the learning they bring about. It is in this sense that causal knowledge is essential in teaching.

This establishes that causal knowledge is necessary for the practice of teaching; it does not tell us what causal knowledge a teacher needs to possess. It is neither in the scope of this work nor in the scope of its author's ability to specify what such knowledge would be. It is helpful, though, to suggest the sorts of knowledge that would be relevant. The work of educational researchers in their studies of teaching is, of course, devoted to filling out this knowledge. The point of much of this research is to locate what actions of teachers are likely to bring about learning. The studies in the "process-product" area of research are examples of this sort of enterprise. Here the product is typically defined as the learning students acquire as measured by some sort of achievement test. Various teacher behaviors, i.e. "processes," are correlated with the achievement scores to determine which behaviors are associated with increased learning. Other variables that might be connected to learning, such as the native ability of the students, will be controlled in such studies so as to try to show that the teacher's actions are not only associated with the increased learning but can be said to cause it. That is, if other possible causal factors can be shown not to be present, the likelihood is increased that the process under consideration is not only correlated with the achievement but is also a cause of the achievement.

To be sure, there are limits to such research. If one does not accept the definition of successful teaching as being represented by the scores students earn on achievement tests, little point would be seen in this line of research. If one defines successful teaching differently though, there will be another kind of product for which one can conduct research to determine which processes are likely to bring about the desired product. As well, one can accept the research but claim that it is not applicable in a certain circumstance. That is, one can believe that a certain process is indeed causally efficacious in bringing about learning but that in the present situation there are good reasons for not attempting to use the process to bring about learning. As will be seen later in more detail, decisions in teaching are made under a variety of constraints that can suggest quite different courses of action. A further limit is that the results of causal investigations may come into conflict with other principles that the teacher is utilizing. In such cases, the teacher may well accept the causal relationship but not employ it because other factors take precedence in the situation. These sorts of points do not give any ground for claiming that there is anything fundamentally wrong or misplaced about this line of research; they allow that research on teaching is one source of information on causal relations in teaching that may be used by teachers to bring about learning.

A brief report on some of this research suggests how it can serve as a causal basis for teaching.

> The process variables correlating most strongly and consistently with achievement were those suggesting maximal student engagement in academic activities and minimal time spent in transitions or dealing with procedures of conduct. . . . [Successful teachers] demonstrated "withitness" by monitoring the entire class when they were instructing, and by moving around during seat work time. They rarely made target errors (blaming the wrong student for a disruption) or timing errors (waiting too long to intervene), although they were more likely than other teachers to be coded as overreacting to minor incidents. Even so, they were more likely than other teachers to merely warn rather than threaten their students, and less likely to use personal criticism as punishment. They were proactive in articulating conduct expectations, vigilant in monitoring compliance, and consistent in following through with reminders or demands when necessary.[9]

Each of these attributes of successful teachers, at least successful in the sense of bringing about achievement, is a competence that one can develop. So, a teacher wishing to do that which is correlated with student achievement can deliberately acquire or improve these competencies. In this way, a teacher can utilize these research results to try to cause greater learning in students. In this way, this knowledge becomes a part of the teacher's fund of causal knowledge.

There are, to be sure, many areas of knowledge that can be used as causal knowledge in teaching. Psychological knowledge about how people learn and what they are capable of doing at various levels of development can be utilized by teachers to bring about the intended learning. Knowledge of social and sociological factors in learning, knowledge of sex and gender differences and knowledge of the social context in which the students are living are all areas that can determine the teacher's causal base of knowledge. A complete catalog of the knowledge that teachers can use to cause learning would be extensive indeed. Given the idiosyncrasies of teachers and their different backgrounds it is, as well, unlikely that any two teachers would share a complete repertoire of such knowledge. It is clear, though, that any teacher will possess some knowledge, or putative knowledge, that is utilized in determining what should be done to help students learn.

Normative knowledge

I take some liberties in describing the topic of this section as "normative knowledge." The point I want to make is that part of the knowledge and beliefs the teacher brings to the intentional situation is of values. To be more precise, I should say that what is brought to the teaching situation is what the teacher claims to know or believes with respect to values as they relate to teaching practice. I shall refer to such claims as the teacher's normative knowledge, and, in doing so, will not commit myself to any position on the question of whether normative claims can have a truth value. The values that teachers hold are used in a variety of ways in their activity as teachers. In research on teachers' thoughts, judgments and decisions, a source of knowledge that is identified is the set of goals a teacher brings to the teaching situation.[10] A goal is, "the teachers' general aim for the task, usually learning and/or affect."[11] Such claims are statements of what teachers believe should be achieved in a teaching situation; they would give the ends to be reached if the teaching were to be successful. As such they do not represent causal claims one could make in teaching, nor would they be immediate statements of observable fact. Goals are standards to be accomplished; they represent what a teacher intends to achieve in teaching. They set the norms for particular teaching situations.

The sources of this knowledge are varied. The teacher can set the goals for teaching independently of external sources. In such cases, the teacher's beliefs about the subject to be taught, the characteristics of the particular students being taught, and the environment of the classroom and school in which the teaching takes place can, and often will, enter into the teacher's decision. Under this view of goal setting, a teacher determining what is to be taught in a fifth grade social studies unit to talented students in an upper middle class school will likely come up with quite different aims than would a teacher teaching fifth grade social studies to learning disabled students. But these factors would not seem to be sufficient in outlining the sources of this knowledge. The teacher's own background, training and experience would enter into the decision process. The particular range of knowledge that a teacher has about the subject matter of fifth grade social studies, what the teacher has learned in formal situations about the teaching of fifth grade social studies, and the experience the teacher has had in the teaching of this subject will all enter into the aims the teacher sets. Variation in any of these areas could be sufficient for the generation of quite different sets of goals to be achieved.

At the other extreme, teachers can rely on external sources for the setting of aims. Instead of deciding independently what the students are to be taught, the teacher can take the goals from other sources. Here, the normative knowledge on which a teacher relies is based on an authoritative statement rather than on the teacher's own evaluation of the situation. The most common sources of authoritative claims about goals in teaching are textbooks, curriculum guides, a school's statements of what is to be learned, and the statements of bodies that have governing authority over the schools. Such documents typically provide the teacher with goals to be achieved and materials and methods for the accomplishment of these goals. These goals are part of the teacher's normative knowledge even though they are accepted, in the same way that reports of fact can be accepted, on the basis of authority. In these cases, the goals are generated by external sources but become the teacher's goals. The teacher accepts them as the aims or norms to be achieved in the teaching situation. They set the teacher's activities as much as if the teacher had generated the goals independently. The social conditions of teaching can lead teachers to accept externally based goals as the determinants of teaching situations. Public education, which is under the control of governments and school districts and which attempts to provide articulation in the overall educational programs of students, will often leave little room for teachers to generate sets of goals for their students which are independent of the social environment in which the teachers find themselves. The conditions under which teachers practice encourage them, to put it mildly, to adopt the goals of the system as their own goals.

That teachers accept external goals as their own is supported by the finding in research on teachers' decision making that "teachers do not follow the traditional model for instructional design by specifying objectives, creating step-by-step procedures for moving students with certain entry skills and knowledge to those objectives, and evaluating the effectiveness of instruction after implementing it. Rather, teachers focus on the activities—content, material—with which students will be involved."[12] In deciding what to do in a classroom, teachers typically begin by thinking of the activities that they want students to engage in, what textbooks, films and other materials to use, what projects might be appropriate to assign. In thinking about activities such as these, teachers are still bringing normative knowledge to bear on the situation even though they may not formulate goals explicitly. In focusing on the material and content to use the teacher is making an indirect decision about what is to be learned. If the possible material to choose is, to keep the choice simple, textbook A or B, the decision the teacher makes will determine what it is that the students will be taught. To the extent that the possible learning that results from book A is different from that in B, the choice of texts will determine what the goals to be achieved are. To be sure, in choosing the text the teacher will take a variety of factors into account such as the suitability of the text for these students and the availability of the text, but one of the factors that will be considered is what can be learned from the textbook. In this way, even though teachers may not as a matter of fact first set objectives for teaching before considering the activities students will engage in, normative knowledge enters into the teacher's deliberations concerning the teaching situation.

Normative knowledge is, then, a necessary component of a teacher's decisions concerning a teaching situation. Because these situations are intentional, they are characterized by the goals that can be achieved in them. A teacher's practice is determined by the norms that are set. Without such norms there would be no point to the enterprise, there would be no way for the teacher to implement the causal knowledge that is held about teaching. So, even though teachers may not focus on norms directly, they must utilize their beliefs about what is to be achieved in teaching in the decisions they make.

Normative knowledge enters the practice of teaching at another level as well. The general claims that teachers take to be true about the whole activity of teaching and the nature of education also enter into their decisions.[13] These would not set the norms for a particular teaching situation in the sense described above where the norms give the learning that one is trying to achieve through teaching. Rather, these beliefs show the general principles to which a teacher is committed in the practice of teaching. The teacher's beliefs about the point of teaching, about the kinds of learning that are most desirable, and about what constitutes an educated person would be kinds of principles that teachers would bring to bear on decisions. Such principles will not give explicit direction to particular teaching situations. A teacher who believes, for example, that learning basic content is the most desirable kind of learning cannot use this principle to determine what should be done in a particular case. But this principle will rule out many possibilities. It would eliminate from consideration the possibility that the teacher might allow the students to choose their own areas of study, for example. These general principles set limits on the range of activities that students will engage in; they determine, as it were, the range of possibilities from which the teacher will choose the particular goals to be achieved. Normative knowledge at this level also is utilized in a teacher's deliberations about what is to occur in the course of teaching practice, but it does so by limiting the range of choices that the teacher can make.

Experiential knowledge

Much of the knowledge a teacher brings to the teaching situation is a product of the teacher's experience. This knowledge cuts across the other kinds of knowledge that have been identified. Some of the teacher's experiential knowledge will be causal, some will be normative, while other components of it, such as knowledge of specific facts, may fit neither of these categories. To characterize some of the teacher's knowledge as experiential knowledge is to identify the source of the knowledge rather than to give its nature. The reason this sort of knowledge is worthy of mention is that it highlights the importance of looking at what the teacher has learned through practice as a part of the corpus of knowledge and beliefs that is brought to bear upon the decisions and judgments of teaching.

The knowledge at issue here has some similarities to what Schön has called reflection-in-action.[14] Reflection-in-action is that knowledge a practitioner reveals in practice in spontaneous ways; indeed, typically it cannot be put in explicit terms. A teacher who changes strategies in the middle of lesson because the original one does not seem to be working is displaying reflection-in-action. The teacher does not stop to think about what to do; it is immediately seen that something must be done and the teacher knows what to do. In most cases, it would seem, that a teacher when asked later why the change was made would be able to give reasons for the change, but in Schön's formulation of this type of knowledge this is not necessary. Even when a teacher makes the right move without being able to explain why, the teacher has demonstrated reflection-in-action. Reflection-in-action would be an instance of experiential knowledge in that this spontaneous knowledge that need not be made explicit would have to be the result of learning in practice. If it were learned independently of practice, one would be able to make it explicit. What one learns in preparation for practice or prior to practice is knowledge that the person can formulate, state or describe, unless of course one's memory fails. It would seem that only in the course of doing something would we acquire knowledge that we can use but not verbalize. So, reflection-in-action is a kind of experiential knowledge.

Reflection-in-action, though, does not exhaust the range of experiential knowledge. What one learns through experience need not only be displayed in spontaneous actions in practice, nor need it remain tacit. Through trial and error one can learn causal relations that obtain in teaching situations. A teacher can learn through experience that reducing class time devoted to routines and increasing class time for instruction can increase student achievement. One need not go to the research literature to discover this; it is the sort of thing one can discover on one's own. It need not be a spontaneous revelation, nor need it be ineffable. Similarly, normative knowledge can be experiential but not a case of reflection-in-action. Through experience one can develop norms or standards that one hopes to achieve in teaching. These can enter the teacher's normative knowledge through experience. Working for the first time with learning disabled children can result in revisions about what one hopes to achieve through one's teaching. That is, the norms the teacher intends to achieve can be modified through the experience of working with children. Again there is nothing spontaneous or ineffable about such learning.

It would seem that experiential knowledge would be an important source of knowledge that teachers bring to bear upon their practice. In the practice of teaching, judgments and decisions are made frequently, as in any profession. Of all the sources of knowledge that can be called upon in the making of these judgments and decisions, the freshest and most recent knowledge would seem to be the most likely to be called upon. Experiential knowledge would seem to have the advantage of being the freshest in the teacher's mind. What one learns through experience has the virtue of being vivid and accessible. As a result experiential knowledge would likely be called upon in the daily decision-making of teachers. This is not to say that experiential knowledge is a particularly reliable source of knowledge. It is often the case that the most expert practitioners are those who are able to base their judgments and decisions on knowledge that is not easily accessible. Diagnosing learning difficulties, as in any case of diagnosis, is often hindered if the diagnostician relies only on fresh, experiential knowledge. The instance being examined may be a quite obscure problem where recent experience is of no help. To think that vivid knowledge is particularly reliable could result in mistaken judgments because a correct assessment of the case at hand may require that obscure and distant knowledge be called upon. So, though experiential knowledge is an important source of knowledge for teachers in their practice, no special importance should be given to it as being a kind of "better" knowledge.

A final issue that needs to be mentioned is the simple intractability of experiential knowledge. What teachers learn through experience is so varied that one finds it difficult to get a grasp on this category of knowledge. I have already mentioned causal and normative knowledge as being kinds of knowledge that can be learned experientially. As well facts about students, schools, and the social environment of schooling can be learned experientially. There seems to be, as well, no reason to exclude the learning of skills from the possibility of experiential learning. Indeed, one suspects that only the learning of highly theoretical and abstract material could not be learned experientially. The reason for this seems to be that such learning requires a great deal of previous learning that must be done in an appropriate sequence before a person can learn the highly abstract material. It seems highly unlikely that this could happen through everyday experience; formal instruction is needed to insure that the appropriate steps are taken. So, the range of knowledge that can be included in experiential knowledge is great indeed. The body of such knowledge that a particular teacher possesses will be a wide assortment of different kinds of knowledge, and there is little reason to suppose that the bodies of knowledge possessed by any two teachers will have much in common. The only thing that one can be sure of is that such knowledge, whatever it might be, will be used by teachers in their practice.

Subject matter knowledge

As teachers are concerned to try to bring about learning, among the sources of knowledge that they will appeal to in their teaching is their knowledge of what they are teaching. I will call this source of knowledge "subject matter knowledge" even though much of the knowledge that might be appealed to in this way would not fit our ordinary understanding of subject matter. A kindergarten teacher, for example, may want to teach students in his class to participate in cooperative activities, a new experience for many children in their first year of school. The knowledge of cooperative activities that the teacher draws upon in his teaching would be part of what I am calling subject matter knowledge even though when we think of school subjects we would not include cooperative activities as one. So, subject matter knowledge in this context is a broad category including formalized arrays of knowledge such as mathematics as well as isolated bits of knowledge that may be taught on an incidental basis. In general, I want to say that subject matter knowledge is that knowledge a teacher possesses of the content of what the teacher intends students to learn. A teacher, in a teaching situation, will intend that students learn X, where X can be anything from cosmology to canasta. Subject matter knowledge, here, is the knowledge the teacher has of X.

Teachers' decisions about their practice rely crucially on subject matter knowledge. The intention to be met by the teaching may or may not be drawn from this knowledge base; the teacher may be presented with an objective that is decided upon independently of the knowledge base the teacher brings to the situation. Once the teacher is faced with the question of what to do to bring about the intention, some recourse to subject matter knowledge seems inevitable. The intention sets the norm to be achieved. The teacher's causal knowledge may well provide empirical evidence about what procedures are likely to bring about the desired end state. There is still no content for the teacher to focus on; it is the store of subject matter knowledge that gives substance to the teaching situation. If the teacher's intention is to bring about some factual or theoretical knowledge, the content of the teaching will have to include elements of that factual or theoretical knowledge. In straightforward didactic teaching, the content will include the very knowledge to be learned; this would be teaching by telling. In more indirect styles of teaching, this would not be the case, but the teacher will have to appeal to subject matter knowledge in order to enable students to have a chance at learning what is desired. In discovery approaches to teaching, teachers have to provide a certain knowledge base so that students can find out for themselves what it is that the teacher intends for them to learn. One cannot see how these indirect approaches to teaching could proceed if the teacher were to make no reference to his or her subject matter knowledge. The students need a starting point; the teacher's subject matter knowledge provides that starting point. Similar points hold if the teacher's intention is for students to achieve some sort of skill knowledge or attitudinal knowledge. What the teacher provides the students to enable them to acquire the skill or attitude will have to be drawn from the teacher's knowledge of the subject area of the skill or attitude.

Subject matter knowledge cuts across the other categories I have identified. Since my concern is not to provide a neat categorization this is not a problem; my concern is to identify the important sources of knowledge for teachers. Subject matter knowledge may include both normative and causal knowledge; as well it may be experiential. One can learn about what one is teaching informally. It is characteristic of much subject matter knowledge that it is learned in formal settings; teacher education programs are typically built around requirements for providing this type of knowledge. Not only is this the case, but teachers see it to be preferable this way. One study asked teachers what should be learned in preparation programs and what should be learned through experience.[15] Nothing was rated higher as being most appropriately learned in pre-service preparation programs than "Understanding one or more subject areas in depth." Not only did teachers see this as being most appropriately learned in formal situations, they also responded that this aspect of their preparation is both important and effectively done by the institutions they attended. Providing the corpus of subject matter knowledge is both important and appropriate for teacher education programs; it seems also to be a place where they can take some credit. It is not, however, the only place where such learning should occur. Teachers, to be effective, need to add to and revise their store of knowledge. What suffices at the preparation level may not be enough to insure successful teaching practice in later years. This topic will be returned to in the next chapter where teacher education will be my main concern. At this point, it is only necessary to highlight that subject matter knowledge is a necessary component of the knowledge base that teachers appeal to in their practice.

General knowledge

The sources of knowledge that I have discussed so far provide the teacher with the specific knowledge that can be appealed to in teaching practice. Normative knowledge is the source for the aims and goals the teacher will attempt to promote. Causal knowledge provides, among other things, knowledge of the empirical relations that show the effects on students of the teacher's actions. Subject matter knowledge provides the content for the teacher's actions. Experiential knowledge provides a further basis in all these areas which the teacher has learned in the course of, and through reflection on, practice. The final type of knowledge I wish to identify is one that is not unique to teachers but does play, I believe, an important and special role in teaching practice. I call this general knowledge.

General knowledge is that knowledge a person has of the world in an undifferentiated, non-specific way. It is the knowledge that one has as a result of living in the world; it is comprised of the information and skills that one acquires in order to live as a reasonably competent and informed person in society. It would include such things as a knowledge of current affairs in one's society, a knowledge of and the ability to function in one's economic system, and an acquaintance with the stories, myths, literature or artistic traditions of one's society. It is the store of knowledge a person possesses that is not restricted to any particular role, function or concern of the individual. It is, rather, the knowledge a person has that one would expect would be shared to a large extent by others with whom the person lives in a social way.

We all possess some general knowledge since it is the knowledge we share with those around us that enables us to interact with our fellow humans. Without any general knowledge, we would not able to communicate with our fellows. In order to communicate we need to share some knowledge with others, we have to know what we are communicating about. The actual body of general knowledge that people have will vary to great extents. The more general knowledge a person possesses the greater the number of others that can be communicated with and the greater the number of topics on which they can communicate. There are, of course, attempts to reform and prescribe the general knowledge that people in a society will possess.[16] I will not try to provide a catalog of such knowledge that is in some way essential or vital. Of course, I, like everyone else, have some ideas on what ought to be included in such a body of knowledge. There are things that I am shocked that others do not know as a matter of course. But the problem inherent in providing such an account is suggested by the further fact that I shock others by what they see as my appalling ignorance of matters that they see as basic. Try, for example, living in a city with a prominent and successful professional hockey team without being much of a hockey fan. The problem I allude to is the inherent relativity of general knowledge to the situation and concerns of the individual. The knowledge that one needs to possess as a reasonably competent and informed member of a society is very much dependent on that society and one's interests within it. To prescribe certain general knowledge as being necessary for everyone is to make a judgment that everyone should have an interest in that knowledge. As a matter of fact, that interest will not be generally shared, so it becomes incumbent on the proponent of standardized general knowledge to show why every individual should be interested in the proposed general knowledge. To do this is no easy task, and one that I will not attempt. The point I am making is a bit more fundamental; it is that everyone must possess some general knowledge in order to be a reasonably competent and informed member of society.

I will, though, attempt a somewhat stronger and more difficult position in looking at the teacher's special role with respect to general knowledge. I will make two points. First, I want to claim that teachers must possess a broad general knowledge. Second, I want to claim that they have the responsibility of enhancing their students' store of general knowledge. My first point is based on the fact that general knowledge is a requirement for communication between people. The teaching situation is one, as has been described, that is an interpersonal situation between the teacher and students. For communication between people to take place there must be some common knowledge shared by them. So, teachers must share common knowledge with students. As it is the teacher that initiates the intentional situation, it would seem to be the teacher's responsibility to have the general knowledge that enables communication with the students. Teachers, under this view, should make themselves aware of what general knowledge is needed to insure that communication in the interpersonal situation of teaching is possible. What, in fact, this general knowledge will be will, of course, vary in may different ways. Teachers working with very young students will require less than teachers working with adults because, in that young children typically have smaller stores of general knowledge than adults, there will be less to be shared with young children. The subject area may as well affect the general knowledge needed by teachers. A teacher whose sole concern is mathematics may well need less than a social studies teacher because to be a reasonably competent and informed member of society would seem to require more information related to social studies than to mathematics. Finally, the teacher's causal knowledge may be a factor involved here. It may be that teachers who share greater amounts of general knowledge are teachers who are more successful in their teaching. If this is so, then this would be a basis for suggesting that teachers' general knowledge needs to be broad enough for this possible causal relation to hold. This is, of course, speculative, but it does suggest how general knowledge can be related to other sources of knowledge. In spite of the variability that will be found in teachers' general knowledge, it is the case that teachers must have some general knowledge.

My second point is that teachers have the responsibility for increasing the students' store of general knowledge. This goes beyond a narrow interpretation of teaching in that it is not required by the concept of teaching; this rather is an educational good that can be achieved by teachers. The teacher creates an intentional situation in which the intention of the teacher to promote some learning defines and gives meaning to the situation for both students and the teacher. What the teacher intends for students to learn may be highly specialized with nothing to do with the corpus of general knowledge. I want to give some plausibility to the notion that, among the teacher's intentions, there should be the intention to help students increase their knowledge of what it is to be a reasonably competent and informed member of society. I base this on the social nature teaching. That teaching is a social activity, one that puts people into interpersonal situations, is a claim I have already supported. Where teaching is a part of a socially supported enterprise, as is clearly the case in public education, one of the interests to be served by education and teaching is to enable and promote the competence of individuals as members of that society. Insofar as teachers are agents of this social enterprise their intentions must include the intention to enable their students to be competent and informed members of society. The intentions of teachers, if successful, to get students to learn specialized knowledge will, of course, increase their competence and information. But this would not necessarily increase the students' general information. To insure this, teachers should intend to teach general knowledge. In this way, the competencies and information students need to be members of their society would be transmitted to them, and a general interest of society in the education of its younger members would be met. This is, of course, not all there is to the education of the young, but in those contexts where education is a social enterprise it would seem to be an essential part.

The utilization of knowledge

With this sketch of teaching as a practice and the knowledge that is appealed to in the course of teaching, the question that I now want to consider is how that knowledge is used in the course of teaching. I have considered a variety of approaches to this question in the early chapters; with the account of teaching that I have presented and the discussion of the practice of teaching and the knowledge base of teaching, I can now develop an account of how knowledge is utilized in teaching, which to me is the central issue in the debate labelled "the relation of theory and practice in education."

The meaning of the teaching situation, I have argued, is created for both the teacher and students by the intention the teacher brings to the situation. With the discussion of the knowledge bases of teaching, we can see the sources of these intentions. Although, in my discussion so far, the actual content of the intentions of the teacher has been left indeterminate, in the course of teaching the intention that the teacher has is of the utmost importance. This omission in my discussion can now be rectified. The intentions that a teacher adopts that give meaning to the teaching situation will be drawn from the teacher's knowledge. The teacher's normative knowledge will be an important, if not the most important, source. What the teacher believes about teaching and education, the desirable end states that can be achieved by students, and the purposes to be served by teaching and education, both for the students themselves and for the society in which the students live or, perhaps, ought to live, will be central in the teacher's choices about what should be achieved as a result of the teaching situation. Normative knowledge can, of course, cover a wide range so that often it will not provide the detail for determining the intention for a particular teaching situation. A teacher may believe that all students should be able to reason critically and thoughtfully about information that is presented to them, or the teacher may hold the opposing belief that students should come to accept the word of authority as presented to them. Whatever side of this issue that teachers come down on, even though I would not maintain that both sides of this divide are equally valid, it is clear that this belief alone is not sufficient to establish an intentional teaching situation. To believe that students should come to be critical and thoughtful reasoners is not enough to establish a plan for what is to be done in the course of teaching. A teaching plan would have to include some content as well. So in a case such as this, the teacher's normative knowledge is not sufficient to establish the teaching situation. To do so, the teacher will have to appeal to subject matter and causal or experiential knowledge. When the teacher takes a belief about what should be accomplished in the teaching situation and adds to it beliefs about what is to be known in a particular area, the steps one can take to bring about this knowledge, and what one has learned by experience; the teacher should have adequate grounds for forming not only an intention for the teaching situation, but also a plan for bringing about that intention.[17] To believe that students should think critically about issues, to know that issue X is in the approved curriculum for these students, to know that performing Y is likely to bring about a critical stance on X, and to know from experience that Y has been successful is to have sufficient background to form the intention that the students should become critical with respect to X as a result of teaching them by doing Y. The teacher's knowledge is, thus, the source of the teacher's intention.

There are, to be sure, cases where the sources of knowledge will be much less wide ranging. The teacher may believe, as a part of one's normative knowledge, that all students should learn two-digit subtraction without regrouping. This alone seems sufficient to establish the intention of the teaching situation. For a teacher with sufficient experience, it may also suffice to provide the plan for carrying out the intention. Subject matter knowledge, too, may suffice to create the intention. The teacher's knowledge of the subject matter, along with a curriculum imperative, may create a teaching situation. The teacher's knowledge of how to titrate, in the context of teaching where there is a set curriculum for students that includes titration, determines that in this teaching situation the intention is for students to learn how to titrate.

The intention which creates the teaching situation is, thus, a function of the knowledge that teachers bring to the situation. In the normal course of affairs, teachers will form intentions for their teaching that are the result of the knowledge that they bring to the situation. What teachers know or believe, in all the forms that this can take, is the source for the intentions that teachers have. If this line is plausible, as I think it is, it suggests a simple story with respect to the utilization of knowledge. Once we see that teaching is characterized by the creation of an intention and that there is a range of knowledge available to teachers through study and experience, we can see how the intention and plan for teaching are developed. It all seems a straightforward business; it may not be routine in that the teacher is expected to decide what should be pursued and such decisions can be very complex. It is not an easy business either; the amount of knowledge that is needed to make these decisions is, as I hope I have made clear, great indeed.

Not only is the formation of intentions for the teaching situation neither routine nor simple, it turns out that it is not straightforward. The discussion so far assumes that the knowledge the teacher brings to the teaching situation is unproblematic. If however, the teacher's knowledge contains beliefs that are not consistent or if the teacher obtains through experience beliefs that contradict other beliefs the teacher has, then the account of how teachers formulate intentions for teaching situations that has been given is no longer applicable. If the teacher's beliefs are inconsistent, then they no longer provide an intention that the teacher can strive for; they would provide two intentions that would be at cross purposes. The issue becomes one of how the teacher revises beliefs. This is a more difficult, and I believe more interesting, story.

To illustrate this problem, consider the following example from Fenstermacher.[18]

> A classroom teacher . . . was asked why she made such extensive use of work stations and learning centers. The teacher based her action on moral convictions about the proper treatment of children. She clearly believes in choice and individualization, and tried to design her classroom to reflect these commitments. As it turns out, her students were not scoring well on end-of-year standardized examinations. The teacher was concerned about the scores, yet also strongly committed to individualization practices. She would not change her practices if the new practices meant a complete overthrow of her beliefs about the nature of teaching. On further inquiry, she stated that, though she had reservations about standardized examinations, her students ought to do better than they did—and she wished they would.
>
> On further discussion, it became apparent to the teacher that she had at

least two major objectives: honoring the unique aspects of each learner, and each learner's acquiring the material presented. She assumed that classroom procedures for individualization would gain both ends. The data she had on hand (standardized test scores) did not support this assumption, though she was reluctant to reconsider the premises in her practical argument for individualization. With reservation, she began to read the process-product literature on teaching effectiveness. The evidence derived from this line of research shows with a fair degree of clarity that the practices this teacher used to effect individualization are not practices typically correlated with uniform gains in acquisition of content assigned.

Two of the teacher's beliefs are indirectly inconsistent. Her belief that the uniqueness of each child should be honored and respected results in teaching practices, the use of work stations and learning centers, that can be shown empirically not to be correlated with high achievement. This conflicts with her belief that students should acquire the content being taught which would be demonstrated by high scores on standardized examinations. The import of the particular line of educational research mentioned is that the teacher cannot have it both ways; she cannot seek to honor the students' uniqueness and strive to maximize their scores on standardized examinations. Her beliefs and knowledge that she brings to the teaching situation are no longer able to set the intention of her teaching. Her two beliefs require conflicting intentions and plans. What this teacher must do is to revise her beliefs and intentions. Only through changing her beliefs will she be able to formulate an intention for the teaching situation. Inconsistent beliefs inhibit the creation of a teaching situation.

There are many ways in which one can change one's beliefs. One can flip a coin to decide which of two inconsistent beliefs to adopt; heads I stress the uniqueness of each learner, tails I seek to maximize standardized test scores. One can consult an astrologer or medium to decide which to adopt. One can seek the advice of a respected person or a person in authority; one can do as one is told. Or, one can reason about the matter to make the decision. It is the latter that I will concentrate on; indeed, I hope I can say that it is the latter that I will, of course, consider. Reasoned change in belief and reasoned change in intention is the central issue, I believe, in the whole concern for the relation of theory and practice in education. The concern about theory and practice is essentially the concern for how a person's knowledge affects what one does and how changes in knowledge result in changes in action. Implicit in the concern for theory and practice is the belief that such applications and revisions of belief be reasonable. If teachers were expected to make their decisions by seeking authoritative voices or by flipping coins, there would be no concern for theory and practice. It is because teachers are expected to make reasoned choices, choices based on theory and knowledge, that we are concerned about the relation between theory and practice. It is when knowledge is not clear in its directions to us that the issue becomes most salient. When a teacher's knowledge is clear and unproblematic, the teacher's decisions about what to do in practice would seem to be straightforward; one takes the knowledge and applies it in the complex way I have described. But, a teacher's knowledge is not likely to remain clear and unproblematic for long. Experience, study and the results of research are all possible sources of new beliefs that are inconsistent with those held by a teacher.[19] The question of how changes in the teacher's beliefs, what we might call the theory, can be made reasonably, and how such changes also change the teacher's intentions, which determine the teacher's practice, now becomes the central concern.

Reasoned change in view is an issue that has both philosophical and psychological aspects. The philosophical aspects are my concern; but the issue, at least in my experience, is one about which philosophers have had little to say. An important and challenging discussion of this issue has been provided by Gilbert Harman in *Change in View*.[20] I want to try to develop some of his ideas to show how they can help us to understand this general issue of how theory is related to practice in teaching.

Harman begins with a distinction between theoretical and practical reasoning. Theoretical reasoning affects one's beliefs; practical reasoning affects one's intentions and plans.[21] This formulation of the distinction is not the same as other formulations one finds, and it is the case here that theoretical and practical reasoning can be intertwined. Changes in intention may well require changes in belief. In establishing an intentional situation, a teacher may have to change beliefs before changing intentions. The teacher whose beliefs include both the desirability of respecting the student's individuality and the desirability of increased scores on standardized examinations will have to decide which belief is to be given priority before an intentional situation can be created. Changes in belief do not necessitate changes in intention. One can change one's beliefs without altering what one plans to do because one may intend to do nothing about the belief. One may change one's beliefs about the historical development of public education, say that it was an attempt to maintain a particular system of social stratification rather than an attempt to illuminate the lives of the young, without this change being reflected in one's practice. So, theoretical and practical reasoning are independent kinds of reasoning even though they can be related.

Although my concern is with Harman's practical reasoning, the reasoned change in intentions, because of the fact that teaching is an intentional situation, I will focus at the outset on theoretical reasoning, the reasoned change in belief, for two reasons. First, as has just been indicated, changes in intention can require changes in belief. Second, the principles of revision of intentions include the principles of revision of belief.

The first point with respect to changes in belief to examine is the basis on which changes in belief can be said to be reasonable. Harman reports that there are "two competing theories of reasoned belief revision,"[22] the foundations theory and the coherence theory. The foundations theory holds that some of a person's beliefs are dependent on other beliefs, that these beliefs are dependent on still others, and so on until one reaches beliefs that require no justification, the so-called "foundational beliefs." Foundational beliefs would seem to include beliefs that are self-evident or truistic; they may also include beliefs that a person takes to be ultimate or final commitments. Beliefs, according to this theory, are reasonable in that they are either basic or depend on other beliefs which are themselves basic or can be shown to depend on basic beliefs. When this theory is adopted, revision to one's beliefs requires that one subtract from one's set of beliefs any belief that is not dependent on basic beliefs, or on other beliefs that are dependent on basic beliefs, and that one would add to one's set of beliefs any belief that is basic, or that can be shown to be dependent on basic beliefs. In essence, this theory states that a person is not justified in holding any belief unless the person can provide the other beliefs or evidence on which the belief is based. A belief is reasonable only if the person has evidence or grounds for it.

The coherence theory holds that beliefs are reasonable, not on the basis of their being dependent on other beliefs and ultimately on foundational beliefs, but rather that beliefs are reasonable on the basis of their relations to other beliefs. Beliefs are expected, in the coherence theory, to be consistent with one another and to exist in a network of relations, of which the principal relations are implication and explanation. This means that the beliefs that one holds are not ordinarily in need of justification; this is needed only when a there is a special challenge to a belief. If new evidence is inconsistent with an existing belief or suggests that a new system of belief is more adequate, simple, explanatory or better in some other sense, then the person has to evaluate his or her beliefs. Belief revision under this view amounts to making the minimal changes necessary in a system of beliefs to restore coherence to one's set of beliefs. A set of beliefs, that is, requires no ongoing justification; when problems are encountered one revises one's beliefs with the least possible change to bring the beliefs back into coherence.

In comparing these two theories, Harman notes that the "key issue is whether one needs to keep track of one's original justifications for beliefs. . . . the foundations theory says yes; the coherence theory says no."[23] In examining these two theories on this issue, Harman finds that the foundations theory is untenable. According to this theory, one must keep track of one's original justifications of a belief so that one's ongoing beliefs have a justificational structure in which some beliefs serve as reasons or justifications for others.[24] If the original justifications are lost, then one has no grounds on which to hold a belief; there is no principle of conservatism allowed in this theory which would say that because a belief is held it is justified. Rather, this view holds that a belief is justified only insofar as the person is able to provide the original justification for the belief. It is this requirement of the theory that makes it implausible. First, there is the practical difficulty; it is impossible for a person to keep track of all the justifications for one's beliefs. Once a belief has come to be accepted, the reasons for the belief tend to be lost. For example, much of the basic or foundational evidence we have for our beliefs is perceptual, we come to believe things that we have seen or heard, but we can hold the belief long after the perceptual evidence has been forgotten. As a result, under the foundations theory, we are unjustified in holding many, if not virtually all, our beliefs. To be so justified, we would have to be able to provide the reasons for our beliefs; having lost the original beliefs we are unable to do so and, as a result, cannot justify our beliefs. So, the foundations theory is not an accurate descriptive theory for the reasoned revision of beliefs.

If it is untenable as a descriptive theory, it might still be the normative theory to which we ought to adhere; that is, it might be valid as an account of how we should defend our beliefs. However, somewhat similar considerations make the view untenable as a normative theory as well. If it is an account of how we should go about defending and revising our beliefs then its injunction to us is to keep track of all our beliefs. This would require individuals to maintain a vast store of beliefs in their memories. To live up to this norm here, we should attempt to remember the original justifications for our beliefs because without them we have no defense for our present beliefs. This would violate Harman's Principle of Clutter Avoidance: "One should not clutter one's mind with trivialities."[25] There is nothing logically wrong in trying to keep track of all the justifications for our beliefs, as is required if we accept the foundations theory as a normative account, even though we recognize that as a matter of fact we will not be able to keep track of such a multitude of beliefs. But it does seem rather pointless to try to adhere to the foundations theory. "It is more efficient not to try to retain these justifications and the accompanying justifying beliefs. This leaves more room in memory for important matters."[26]

The coherence theory is much more adequate as a descriptive account of how people revise beliefs. The coherence theory does not require that one keep track of one's original justifying beliefs which, as already noted, is in accord with our experience. As well, the coherence theory has a Principle of Conservatism implicit in it: "One's present beliefs are justified just as they are in absence of special reasons to change them."[27] The theory conserves one's present beliefs; they need only be considered when challenged. This is, of course, unlike the foundations theory, which is quite radical in requiring that every belief be justified at all times. Finally, Harman presents the results of psychological studies on belief perseverance, which provide evidence that the coherence theory, rather than the foundations theory, is the theory which actually accounts for the ways people hold on to beliefs.[28] The beliefs we hold are justified in the absence of the original reasons. We are in the position of having to revise our beliefs when there is special reason to do so. We then make the minimal changes required to bring our beliefs back into coherence. This does reflect the way we act. Consider, again, the teacher whose beliefs about respecting the individuality of students came into conflict with her belief that those students should earn high scores on standardized examinations. In the first instance, the teacher was not prepared to change her practices if the new practices meant a complete overthrow of her beliefs about teaching. She was, that is, willing to persevere in her actions even though there was some evidence suggesting that one of her goals could not be met under her original beliefs. If the foundations theory were an adequate account of practice, the teacher would have to stop those practices as soon as it became clear that there was some question. But the teacher did not give up the beliefs when it was seen that the original justification was no longer adequate. Instead, the beliefs continued to be held in a way that shows the conservatism of belief. After further discussion, when the counter-evidence was apparently made stronger, the teacher did begin to question the original beliefs. At this point the reasons for challenging the original beliefs became clearer and so created the need for the teacher to reconsider her beliefs. We are not provided with the end of the story, so we do not know how the teacher revised her beliefs; but the story that is given is reflected much more adequately by the coherence theory than by the foundations theory.

The coherence theory is the better candidate as a descriptive theory of how people revise their beliefs; is it the better candidate as a normative theory? This is established by considering two normative principles of belief revision, one implied by the coherence theory and one by the foundations theory. The theory that contains the more plausible of the principles will be the more plausible normative theory. The coherence theory implies the Principle of Positive Undermining: "One should stop believing P whenever one positively believes one's reasons for believing P are no good."[29] The foundations theory implies the Principle of Negative Undermining: "One should stop believing P whenever one does not associate one's belief in P with an adequate justification (either intrinsic or extrinsic).[30] From what I have said, the latter implication is, I think, clear. A few words, however, are needed to make the former implication clear. In the coherence theory, beliefs do depend on other beliefs. It is not the case in the coherence theory that a belief is justified because one has a continuing record of all the beliefs on which it depends, but this does not mean that a belief does not depend on other beliefs. One can identify the prior beliefs that are most crucial for adding the new belief to one's ongoing set of beliefs. If it turns out that the beliefs that were most crucial in establishing a new belief are unfounded, and one is fully aware of this, then it would be inconsistent to hold that the belief is true and that the grounds for that belief are unfounded. Learning that the grounds for a belief are unfounded, that is, undermines the belief. So, in the coherence theory beliefs are undermined in the way stated by the Principle of Positive Undermining.

Of these two principles, the Principle of Positive Undermining is the more plausible. The reasons for the implausibility of the Principle of Negative Undermining have already been alluded to. It says that when one loses track of the justification of one's belief one should give that belief up. This is implausible as it requires that we give up most of our beliefs. Indeed, there is a good reason not to keep track of one's beliefs; to do so requires attention to the justification tracks of so many beliefs that reasoning would be inefficient and restricted to trivialities. So, of the two principles the Principle of Positive Undermining is the more plausible, and, thus, the theory of which it is part is the more plausible. On these grounds the coherence theory is adopted as the better theory on the grounds that it is both the more accurate as a descriptive theory and more useful as a normative theory.

An important part of Harman's argument, but rather more peripheral to mine, is Harman's argument that "the theory of reasoning must not be confused with logic"[31] By logic Harman means formal deductive logic and inductive logic based on probability theory. His argument is in two parts, one for each type of logic. In considering deductive logic, he points out that if it were relevant to a theory of reasoned belief revision, it would be so by some principles relating logical implication and logical inconsistency to change in belief. He provides such principles,[32] but shows that there are counter-examples to them and that they would only apply to someone who recognized the implication or inconsistency. The upshot for Harman is that formal logic has no special relevance to the theory of reasoning. It is possible that in some cases of theoretical reasoning formal logic will show that a particular belief should not be held; but the fact that formal logic may have a role to play in certain instances of reasoning does not establish that it has a special role to play in all cases of reasoning. As well, Harman recognizes that notions of immediate implication and immediate inconsistency have roles to play in theoretical reasoning. By these he apparently means that the person involved in reasoning has to see the implications and inconsistencies in a set of beliefs for the person to engage in reasoned change in belief. For example, much later he appends the adjective "psychological" to these notions.[33] As well, part of his argument that logic is of no special relevance to reasoning depends on the fact that logical implication can hold between two claims even though the person may not be aware of it. That is, P may imply R by a long intervening argument of which one is completely unaware; but it would be absurd to say that P is the person's reason for holding R because P implies R. In reasoning, the reasons a person holds are in the person's mind. So, the kind of implication that is of interest to Harman is immediate implication that is a kind of psychological notion. This is part of Harman's insistence that implication and inference be distinguished.[34] One of his counter-examples may help: if a person believes P, and that if P then Q, by logical implication the person must believe Q; but, in belief revision, the appropriate inference to make might be to revise one's belief in P, or if P then Q, on the basis of one's belief that Q is not true. By means of examples such as this and detailed discussion Harman concludes that formal logic is not of special relevance to reasoned revision of beliefs.

Another imaginative argument is used to show that inductive logic based on probability theory is also not of special relevance to reasoned revision of belief. He argues that using probability theory to update the probabilities of statements in the light of new evidence results in a "combinatorial explosion" that makes it impossible for people to calculate the required probabilities.[35] Instead, he holds that beliefs must be held on a yes/no basis; that is, whether one either believes a claim or not, it is practically impossible for people to assign probabilities to their beliefs. Again, the argument is more sophisticated than this quick summary suggests, but the lessons of the argument are important.

In separating his particular theory of reasoning (that of reasoned revision of belief) from logic, it is made clear that the revising of belief does not require the use of the techniques of formal logic or of probability theory. A person engaged in the revision of beliefs does not have to keep track of the claims that logically imply one's beliefs, nor does one have to keep track of the probabilities of one's beliefs. Indeed, the thrust of Harman's argument here, as I see it, is that to make logic part of the theory of reasoning is to make the theory impossible to use. In excluding these logical notions from the theory of reasoning, he also suggests what must be included. One must use immediate implication and immediate inconsistency. One needs to see the relations between the beliefs with which one is working. That one does not need to use formal logic does not eliminate the need for the person to check one's beliefs for consistency or for relations of implication. Although one is not required to assign probabilities to one's beliefs, one does need to assign a "yes or no" value to them, to decide whether to accept the claim or not. These basic points that have connections to our understanding of logic, even though they are not the same notions that are to be found in deductive or inductive logic, are, indeed, essential to reasoned revision of beliefs.

Before turning to the revision of belief there is one further preliminary: the implicit commitments one has with respect to one's beliefs. There are two distinctions that are made here. First, one can accept a belief fully or one can accept a belief as a working hypothesis. To accept a belief fully is to take the claim as true. In such a case one is justified in accepting the belief and the evidence on which it is based. If one is so justified then one is justified in having ended one's inquiry into the truth of the claim. A fully accepted belief is one on which the person has closed inquiry. A belief one accepts as a working hypothesis is one accepted for limited purposes. One does not see the belief as true or as one on which further investigation has ended. One uses a working hypothesis because it is useful or fruitful in a certain context, not because it is true. The result of using a working hypothesis may be that it becomes fully accepted if it turns out to be true and further inquiry into its justification can be closed. Alternatively, it may be dropped if it is not true or if it is not useful. It should be noted that to accept a hypothesis fully is not to be dogmatic; although inquiry into the claim is closed, it is not closed forever. It can be reopened if there is sufficient reason to do so.

The second distinction is between accepting a claim for oneself and accepting a claim as a member of a group. This distinction is the same as expressions of merely personal opinion and authoritative statements. To use Harman's example, the difference here is the difference between, "My present intention is to be at the party" and "I promise to be at the party."[36] In the first case, one merely states one's intention; one would not be criticized for later having changed one's mind, given a change in the situation. In the second case, one has made an authoritative statement that others can rely on; one would be criticized for failing to attend the party even if there had been a change in the situation. To be sure, one can promise to attend a party and legitimately fail to attend, but the situations that justify not attending the party when one has promised are much narrower than when one has merely stated one's intention to attend. Promising provides an authoritative basis for the claim that is not provided when one states one's opinion. When one expresses one's opinion, one is accepting the claim only for oneself; when it is expressed authoritatively, one is expressing it for one's group. That is, an authoritative statement is one for which one has evidence that would hold for others as well as for oneself. The clearest cases of this, Harman claims, are to be found in group investigations such as a team of scientists working on a problem or a team of detectives working on a case.[37] In such cases, one should not accept for the group unless one is confident that there is no relevant evidence that one has not considered that is available to the rest of the group. The evidence available to the community, that is, must be taken into account when one is making a claim that is to be authoritative for the community. In expressing one's opinion, on the other hand, one need not be concerned about the evidence available to others.

Of the four possible ways in which beliefs can be accepted, the one of concern here is fully accepted beliefs that are authoritative. In the teaching situation, we are primarily concerned with beliefs that are fully accepted, beliefs on which the teacher has closed inquiry because they are seen to be justified in light of the evidence. The established beliefs of the teacher, in short, are taken to be true. The practice of teaching, as I have tried to suggest, is determined by the teacher's sources of knowledge, those beliefs about norms, subject matter, causal relations and the like that the teacher brings to the teaching situation. In these terms, they would be beliefs that the teacher takes as fully accepted. To be sure, teachers will entertain working hypotheses; they will suspend their beliefs about the truth of a claim to see if it is useful or fruitful in a certain context; but the central issue with respect to the relation of knowledge and practice occurs when what the teacher fully accepts is challenged. The difficult cases, that is, arise when what one takes to be true is seen to be in need of revision. This is the case when the teacher's commitment to the belief is one of full acceptance. Further, since the teaching situation is one involving both teacher and students, the teacher's beliefs are authoritative. They are meant to be accepted by the group, that is, by the teacher and students. Again, teachers will express some beliefs as personal opinion, but these typically are not matters which teachers intend students to learn. The aims of teaching become aims for the students, the subject matter is to be learned by the students, the causal knowledge may be related to how students best learn. All of these claims involve the group and so are to be accepted by the group. So, the beliefs of interest in the teaching situation are fully accepted beliefs that are authoritative.

In fully accepting beliefs in an authoritative way, a person is making four commitments about those beliefs.[38] In holding a belief in this way, one is, first, committed to the claim that one has, or had, sufficient reasons for believing the claim that did not rely on false assumptions. This commitment reflects the Principle of Positive Undermining: that one is justified in holding a belief unless there is the discovery that one or more of the claims on which it rests is false. The second commitment is that when one infers that something is so, there is no significant chance that one's conclusion is false, given one's reason for it. This commitment reflects what Harman calls "objective likelihood." This means that when one believes a claim fully and authoritatively, one believes that the evidence one used in coming to the belief is reliable, or, in other words, the chances of the evidence being misleading or false are small. The third commitment is that in ending inquiry into a claim, one is committed to the claim that further inquiry into the claim should not affect one's conclusions. This commitment stems from what it means to accept a claim fully. The last commitment is that, in accepting a belief as a member of a particular group, a person is committed to the claim that evidence that would affect one's conclusions is not possessed by others in the group. This commitment stems from what it means to accept a belief authoritatively and reflects the social nature of most inquiry. These, then, are the commitments that are implicit in our beliefs that are held fully and authoritatively. The teacher who holds that teaching should respect the individuality of the child is implicitly holding that her reasons for coming to this claim do not rely on any false assumptions, that the likelihood of her being wrong is small, that there is no further need to inquire into the truth of her belief, and that others in her community do not hold evidence on this matter that she does not.

Without these commitments one could not hold a belief authoritatively and fully. Of course, one can be mistaken in these commitments. One can hold, that is, that the justification for one's belief does not rely on any false assumptions when, in fact, it does. It is, thus, when one of these commitments is challenged that the person must engage in theoretical reasoning, the reasoned revision for one's belief. So the implicit commitments also show the sources of criticism that may lead to the revision of beliefs. We have to face the question of revising our beliefs when one or more of the implicit commitments is no longer accepted. A belief is challenged when it is claimed that it relies on a false assumption, that there is a significant chance that one's conclusion is false, that the matter is open to further inquiry, or that others in the group hold relevant evidence that one has not considered. So, the implicit commitments also suggest the basis for changes in one's beliefs. The principles for making any such changes reasoned changes now need to be considered.

Harman, at one point, describes belief revision analogically: "Belief revision is like a game in which one tries to make minimal changes that improve one's position. One loses points for every change made and gains points for every increase in coherence. One does not normally try to maximize. One tries to get a 'satisfactory' improvement in one's score."[39] This description gives all the points about belief revision that need to be clarified. Losing points by making changes alludes to several principles, but mainly the Principle of Conservatism. This states that, "One is justified in continuing to accept something fully in the absence of special reason not to."[40] This principle is an outgrowth of the coherence theory, which says that beliefs stand in need of justification only when challenged rather than that beliefs always stand in need of justification. The Principle of Positive Undermining, which states that one should stop believing P whenever one positively believes one's reasons for believing P are no good, gives the criterion for having a special reason not to continue to accept a belief fully. Finally, the four commitments in accepting a belief fully and authoritatively give the criteria for what counts as believing that one's reasons are "no good." If one positively believes that a belief depends on a false assumption, that there is a significant chance that one's conclusion is false given the reasons one has for it, that inquiry into a belief is possible, or that there is evidence for a belief that one does not have that others in one's group do have, then one believes that one's reasons are no good.

Another principle is appealed to here as well, the Principle of Interests:

"One is to add a new proposition P to one's beliefs only if one is interested in whether P is true (and it is otherwise reasonable for one to believe P)."[41] The role of this principle is not clear to me. It seems that its purpose is to limit the range of possible beliefs a person may entertain. By limiting the candidates for beliefs that one will accept to those that one is interested in, one will perhaps avoid the problem that the Principle of Clutter Avoidance seeks to prevent, that the person will become burdened with trivialities. Also, to restrict new beliefs to those one is interested in seems to reinforce the conservatism of the position; there are limits to the range of ideas one will consider. The problem with this, and which makes the purpose of this principle less than clear, is that Harman immediately says that "the interest need not be a strong one; it could be a trivial whim."[42] If the point of the Principle of Interest is to limit a person's range of possible new beliefs to avoid cluttering one's mind, it does seem at least odd that the principle would allow trivial whims to be added to one's beliefs. Although the role of this principle is not clear, it does seem to be the case that in this part of the game of belief revision it is the Principle of Conservatism that carries the weight.

The Principle of Conservatism puts the burden of proof on those who would challenge one's beliefs. A person is justified in continuing to accept a belief fully unless there is a clear and positive challenge to that belief. If the challenge, in one of the four ways indicated, cannot be made there is no reason to drop the belief. Belief revision is, as this principle's name suggests, a conservative activity; we continue to hold our beliefs over the course of time; we have to be pushed and prodded into revising our beliefs. In the game of belief revision, we try to avoid having to change our beliefs; we lose points when we are forced into doing so. But, we are, after all, human; we do make mistakes. We sometimes accept false assumptions. We do not always take into account all the evidence available. Our evidence may not be reliable. In sum, we may hold beliefs for which there are special reasons not to hold them. No matter how careful we are in formulating our beliefs, there will be cases where we have to change our beliefs. Even though we try not to lose points by having to change beliefs, there are times when we will. How do we get those points back?

We get them back by improving the coherence of our beliefs. There are two elements for improving coherence that are given: avoiding inconsistency and seeking explanatory coherence. These are not identified as principles as is the case with the conservative side of belief revision; why they are not is not clear to me. Harman says that "coherence is reflected in one's disposition to avoid inconsistency and a tendency to promote explanatory and implicational connections among one's beliefs."[43] It may be that in describing the features of the coherence side as tendencies and dispositions, he believes that these are natural properties of persons in the way that sugar, other things being equal, has the tendency to dissolve when stirred into tea (another of Harman's examples). If this is what he means, and it is speculation on my part that he does, it should be resisted. Why conservatism should be a principle, a norm that we should follow, and avoiding inconsistency should be a natural tendency is not a difference that is clear, much less justified. Indeed, one suspects that people would only acquire the disposition to avoid inconsistency by first heeding an injunction that one should avoid it. A person needs to learn the problems and pitfalls in being inconsistent and that one should do one's best not to make this kind of mistake. It does not seem to be a natural psychological property of humans. I will then take the liberty to refer to the Principles of Avoiding Inconsistency and of Seeking Explanatory Coherence.

In discussing inconsistency, Harman claims that, "One always has a reason to be interested in avoiding inconsistency."[44] Although belief revision is dependent to some extent on the interests of the person, as stated by the Principle of Interests, one cannot announce that one is not interested in consistency. This is an interest that cannot be avoided. The reason is, of course, implicit in the coherence theory that has been adopted; inconsistent beliefs are quite simply incoherent. To believe both P and not-P is to believe something that makes no sense. If one believes a claim and its negation one might as well believe nothing. As long as one wants to make sense one has an interest in avoiding inconsistency. In that we are dealing with reasoned revision of belief, this principle must govern the revisions that one makes. Harman breaks down this principle into two parts: one needs to avoid both immediate and indirect inconsistency. Immediate inconsistency involves blatant instances like the one just mentioned, believing both P and not-P. Indirect inconsistencies are those that are less obvious. P and Q are indirectly inconsistent if Q happens to imply not-P. One must avoid inconsistencies in both cases. One needs not only to avoid believing two statements that contradict one another, one also needs to check the implications of one's beliefs to assure that they do not lead to inconsistencies.

The Principle of Seeking Explanatory Coherence is much more complex, and a complete account would take me too far afield. Indeed, I do not think that one could say that Harman provides a complete account in this work. I shall try to make clear some basic points about explanatory coherence. First, some preliminary points need to be made. The concern for coherence is to show that one's beliefs fit into a network in which one's beliefs are related by explanation and implication. Part of Harman's concern is to suggest that relations of implication may be special cases of relations of explanation. His conclusion on this point is very tentative: "This does not absolutely establish that the relevance to reasoning of implication is a special case of explanatory coherence, but it indicates that this may be so or at least that it may be possible to say this without stretching language too far."[45] Without taking sides on this issue, I will treat relations of explanation and relations of implication as independent, but for ease of reference will include both under my label of the Principle of Explanatory Coherence. Second, Harman limits the term "explanation" to refer to something one understands that makes one's view more coherent and intelligible; he is not using the word to refer to the speech act of explaining. Further, the relevant explanations will always be ones which explain why or how something is so. This excludes such explanations as those explaining what a word means or who someone is.[46]

Several ways in which explanatory coherence might obtain are identified. Two beliefs might be related because the explanation between them is immediately intelligible. That is one might believe that P, that Q and that P because Q on the grounds that the relation between P and Q is immediately intelligible. His example is believing that this is an emerald and that all emeralds are green on the one hand and that this is green on the other hand. In such straightforward cases the coherence between the beliefs is evident.

A second sort of explanatory coherence is provided by an inference to a best explanation. This "occurs when one infers something that might explain the evidence. One starts by believing e and comes to believe e because h."[47] A teacher believes that a child is not able to learn the material being presented. The teacher explains this by inferring that the child suffers a hearing impairment. The impairment can explain the child's failure to learn. This would be the best explanation if it is the best of the competing explanations for e. What constitutes an explanation and the criteria for determining which of the possible explanations is the best is a difficult and controversial matter.[48] It is sufficient here to leave the details of the matter vague, because, whatever the details, we can see that the best explanation will provide coherence to one's beliefs. As explanations promote understanding and intelligibility, the best explanation will add to the coherence of one's beliefs. When one is in the position of having to revise one's beliefs, because the reasons for holding the belief have turned out to be no good, one may have to find an explanation for a new belief. If the explanation that one is able to infer is one that promotes understanding, it will fit in, or cohere with, the other beliefs that one has that have not been challenged. In this way the explanation that one infers not only adds to the coherence of one's beliefs but also, because it does not challenge other beliefs, will allow other beliefs to be conserved. So, in seeking the best explanation, we not only explain the event at hand, but, by making the event intelligible within our set of beliefs, we minimize the changes in our beliefs that are necessary. Thus, inferring the best explanation adds points by increasing coherence.

Another sort of explanation that fits under the Principle of Explanatory

Coherence is the inference from an explanation. "One starts by believing e and comes to believe h because e."[49] From the teacher's intention to teach two-place subtraction without replacement, one infers that his next mathematics class will deal with subtraction. Again, as the explanation promotes understanding, it will increase the coherence of the person's set of beliefs.

Finally, relations of implication promote coherence. As already noted, Harman suggests that this may turn out to be a special case of explanation. But, whether it does or not, beliefs that a person has that stand in a relation of implication are more coherent than those that do not. A student asks why Oslo is the capital of Norway; the teacher, interpreting this as a query about what it means for something to be the capital of a country rather than as an historical question about Norway, responds by saying that the seat of the Norwegian government is to be found in Oslo. That the seat of the Norwegian government is in Oslo implies that it is the capital of Norway, but it does seem odd to say that it explains why it is the country's capital. There is a relation of implication between these beliefs which provides coherence to the student's beliefs even though we do not seem to have an explanatory relation here.

In sum, then, beliefs are revised when there is special need to do so. The criteria for reasoned revision of belief are that one tries to keep as many beliefs as possible without change by the Principle of Conservatism, and that the beliefs that are changed are done so to avoid inconsistency and to add explanatory coherence by the Principle of Coherence. So far, I have dealt with reasoned change of belief. As I stated earlier, my primary concern is with reasoned change of intentions, that is with practical reasoning. Fortunately, not too much has to be added to the account; the Principles of Conservatism and Coherence apply to reasoned change of intention as well. All that I need to do now is to say a few words about Harman's notion of intention and to add one further principle, the Principle of Desire Satisfaction.

Intentions are, for Harman, an independent kind of mental state; they are not implicit in ordinary beliefs and desires. The difference here is seen by counter-example. One may believe that giving a lecture on the causes of World War I will result in the students' learning this; one may desire that students learn this. But, if one is practicing the lecture in the staff room while the intercom system has been left on, unknown to the teacher, in such a way that the students hear the rehearsal and learn the causes of World War I, we would not say this was a case of intentional teaching even though the teacher desired that students learn this and believed that delivering the lecture would enable students to learn it. Intending something, thus, cannot be reduced to believing that something and desiring it. This point is important methodologically in that, if intentions could be reduced to beliefs and desires, there would be no category of practical reasoning; all questions could be subsumed under reasoned change of belief.

The second preliminary point is to note that Harman claims that all intentions, at least all positive intentions,[50] require a plan. If one intends to do A, one must have some idea, perhaps quite dim, of how A will be brought about. A person who claims to intend A but reports that he has absolutely no idea about how A will come about is a person whom we would suspect is not sincere in his intention. A teacher who intends for students to learn some subject matter has a plan on how to realize the intention. In some cases, the plan will be quite explicit; in the case of experienced teachers, only a sketch of a plan might be thought out with the details to be filled in from experience as the teacher works through the teaching. In any case, there will be some plan. In that the plan is itself intended, the plan is part of the intention. So, the revision of intentions also involves the revision of plans. This incidentally is another difference between intentions and desires. Desires require no plans. One who desires to win the Nobel Prize need not have a plan for doing so. One who intends to win it must have a plan; a person who has no plan for winning the Nobel Prize cannot be said to intend to win it. Harman has much more to say about intentions, much of it important and interesting, some of it quite obscure, but I will now turn to one additional principle needed for an account of revising intentions.

Three principles are provided for reasoned change in intention: Conservatism, Coherence and Desire Satisfaction. The first two are adaptations of the parallel principles of reasoned change in belief. In my reading of Harman, I find nothing said about the Principle of Conservatism except that it says "to minimize changes in one's intentions."[51] Presumably, the reasons for this principle are similar to those for the parallel principle in theoretical reasoning. That is, an appeal to the coherence theory of justification which would say that one is justified in doing what one intends to do unless there is some special challenge to the intention and an appeal to a higher level principle on the need to avoid cluttering one's mind with intentions would serve to justify the Principle of Conservatism in practical reasoning.

Rather more is said about the Principle of Coherence, "which encourages changes that would make one's intentions more coherent with each other and with one's beliefs and which discourage changes that would make them less coherent."[52] In support of this principle, it can first be noted that the avoidance of inconsistency is just as important here as it is in the case of theoretical reasoning; it is inconsistent to intend to do both A and B if one believes that one cannot do both. To be coherent, a person must give up either A or B as his or her intention. So, the avoidance of inconsistency is required for coherence in intentions. Another aspect of coherence is in the relation of the intention and its plan. Positive intentions, those intentions that involve the thought that having the intention to do A will lead one to do A, require that one have a plan for doing A, as already noted. So, in the case of positive intentions, one is unjustified in intending to do A if one has no idea how one will do it.

For a positive intention to be coherent, it must have a concomitant plan. Harman offers no analog, at least in my reading, to the requirement of explanatory coherence that is given for coherence of beliefs. In speculating why this is so, if my reading is correct, it seems that this might be due to fact that intentions are an independent state of mind and not reducible to beliefs or desires. Explanations are of events or states of affairs. If we were to explain one's intentions, we would have to see the intention as an event in a person's life. To do so, it seems we would have to regard the intention as a kind of belief. Suppose a teacher intends to promote the student's individuality as a learner. If we were to attempt to explain why the teacher has this intention, we would provide reasons or evidence why or how the teacher came to have this intention which would seem to amount to explaining why the teacher believes this is what should be achieved through teaching. This treats the intention as a belief and so is contrary to the basic distinction on which practical reasoning is based. To be sure, when one has an intention, one will also have beliefs about that intention. This does not mean that intentions and beliefs are not independent mental states; it only says that theoretical and practical reasoning will be intertwined. Explanatory coherence seems applicable only on the theoretical side of this intertwining. So, it may not be appropriate to have an analog for it in practical reasoning.

The Principle of Desire Satisfaction is the additional principle required for practical reasoning. This principle, "encourages changes that promise to promote the realization of one's ends and which discourages changes that promise frustration of these ends."[53] In practical reasoning, the desire that an intention be true is a legitimate ground for adopting it, as this principle recognizes. This is, of course, contrary to theoretical reasoning where the desire that a belief be true is not grounds for accepting the belief. Harman has little more to say on this principle directly, but says quite a bit more indirectly. By this I mean that he devotes an entire chapter to an issue raised by this principle but in which he never mentions the principle. The issue raised deals with the extent or range of one's ends and is dealt with under the rubric of intended and merely foreseen consequences. In general, when one intends to do E, some end state, by means of M, some plan, there will be side effects S of doing M and further consequences C of achieving E. For example, the teacher who establishes learning centers (M) to promote individual learning on the part of the students (E) will also prevent their scores from being as high on standardized examinations as if she had taught by more direct means (C) and in the course of establishing learning centers she will have a classroom that is more noisy than one where students work on their own (S). The issue here is whether the person's intention to E includes the consequences and side effects as well. After all, it is plausible to say that, since the teacher intended to promote individuality and since this results in lower scores on standardized examinations, the teacher intended to have the lower scores. But this plausibility quickly breaks down. Suppose a teacher is successful in this intention and the child comes to have an individual way of learning. Suppose further that the child moves to Japan, where it is my understanding that individual learning styles are not encouraged,[54] and the child fails in school in Japan. It seems quite implausible to say the teacher intended for the child to fail school in Japan. We have here a situation where the Principle of Clutter Avoidance, or something like it, is relevant. To include all the consequences and side effects in one's intention is to introduce an unmanageable number of possibly trivial consequences into the intention. On the basis of this and other considerations Harman rejects the "holistic" view of intention. He concludes that the person's intention gives one's ultimate desire, at least in that context, and that the means to that intention give one's instrumental desire, and that side effects and merely foreseen consequences do not need to enter one's deliberations of desires unless, as he says, "they set off alarms."[55] If in one's reflection about one's intentions, one notices that one or more of the foreseen consequences are undesirable, they may require the person to alter one's desires. Such consequences do not require that one alter one's desires; the desire for E may be so strong that one is willing to pay a price in the way of the consequence. In the case that I have been using, the foreseen consequence of lower scores on standardized examinations did set off an alarm in the teacher whose end it was to promote individuality. As the case was described, the alarm "got louder" for the teacher so that she had to rethink her desires, although the case as originally presented did not reveal whether she altered her desires.

The effect of these principles, particularly the Principle of Desire Satisfaction when it is construed in this non-holistic way, is to keep reasoned change of intention as simple as possible. A person would base one's intentions on one's desires where the intention itself is seen as the ultimate desire. One treats one's desires in a simple "yes or no" fashion; a decision is made whether the intention is worth pursuing. One need not assign weights or in some fashion qualify intentions in light the foreseen consequences of acting on the intention. Rather, one simply deals with the intention itself. The foreseen consequences enter into the deliberation when one or more sets off an alarm. At that point, one would examine the intention in light of the alarm and either continue or discontinue the original intention. So, intentions are based on desires and revised when the consequences of acting on them are serious enough to defeat them. In revision of intentions, the Principle of Coherence enters as well so that the revised intention is seen to be coherent with the other beliefs and intentions of the person.

In summary, Harman has provided an account of reasoned change of belief and intention that gives us a way of setting normative standards for the changes that a person makes in what is to be believed or what is to be done. It is an account which in the first instance stresses the continuity and utility of our beliefs and plans. It also is an account that focuses attention on what is important. By ruling out trivial matters and by appealing to the person's interests, it insures that individuals will engage in debate about matters that are of central concern to their lives. We do not stand in a position of continually having to justify our claims and actions; rather once a belief or plan is adopted as justified it remains so until it is challenged or thrown into doubt. At that point, the person has to engage in deliberation to determine if reasoned change of belief or intention is needed. The coherence of one's beliefs and intentions is the central criterion in making such changes. One tries in all cases to avoid inconsistency. One should try to adopt ideas that fit in with other unchallenged beliefs and intentions. The relevant ways of fitting are by relations of implication and, importantly in the case of beliefs, by relations of explanation. When new claims are explained by other beliefs one holds or when they explain other beliefs, they are more properly adopted as beliefs. Finally, in the case of reasoned change in intentions, the position requires that one examine alternatives in terms of the desires that one has with respect to the actions that are proposed. To be sure, there is much that is controversial about this account. There is as well much more that needs to be said. The individual principles can all be clarified to a much greater extent. As well there is much unsaid that probably should be said. To ignore questions of the formation and maintenance of beliefs is to omit much of what is needed to understand change in belief.[56] But this does serve as a conceptual framework for beginning to understand the relation of theory and practice.

Theory and practice

The discussion of this chapter provides a conceptualization of the relation of theory and practice that I would like now to bring together. The question of how theory and practice are related in education can be seen as the question of how the teacher's knowledge is used in daily life and practice. It is not enough for teachers to have knowledge about students, subject matter and the processes of teaching, or in the case of teacher education for intending teachers to be provided with such knowledge. The knowledge that they have should be reflected in what they do; it should be translated in some way into the actions they perform with students when teaching. This commitment implies that teachers should change what they do when what they believe is inconsistent with what they intend. Further, to be concerned about the relation of theory and practice is to be committed to the view that one's actions should be informed by knowledge. If knowledge had no relevance to what one does, we would not think that theory had any relevance at all to practice. So, the concern for theory and practice implies that changes in what one does should be reasoned changes. The debate, then, about theory and practice in education comes down to the nature of teaching as a practice, the nature of the knowledge that a teacher has, and the nature of reasoned change in belief and intention. These have been my three concerns in this chapter.

The nature of the practice of teaching contributes to our understanding of the issue of theory and practice by showing us that questions about the practice of teaching are decided by teachers in their attempts to achieve the internal goods of teaching. These goods will provide the substance of the content of education that teachers are trying to provide. It establishes as well that teaching is a social and cooperative activity that is conducted in accord with rules and in light of standards of excellence.

The rules and standards of teaching are to be found in the knowledge base that the teacher brings to practice. What I have called a knowledge base is really a collection of disparate elements: actual knowledge, beliefs that the teacher accepts as knowledge which may turn out not to be knowledge, norms and values that one accepts, and what one has picked up through experience. The tradition of the practice determines the knowledge, values, and even lore that become the possession of the teacher in her or his life as a participant in teaching situations with students. In much of the teacher's practice, this knowledge base will suggest unambiguously what is to be done. The knowledge will provide the teacher with clear indications of what can be done to promote the learning of the students. But not always. The beliefs the teacher has may suggest a variety of courses of action. Knowledge might be obtained that is inconsistent with beliefs that are held by the teacher. Through thought and discussion the norms a person holds in teaching may be changed. In these cases, the knowledge base no longer serves as an unambiguous source of direction for the teacher.

When this occurs, the teacher will need to entertain the possibility of changing his or her beliefs. On the presupposition that such changes be rational, it is here that one engages in reasoned change of belief and intention. The principles discussed above provide criteria that the teacher can use when deliberating about such cases to insure that the proposed changes are both necessary and reasoned. These principles are, thus, principles for applying theory to practice. They answer the concern that we have when we raise the question of how theory and practice might be related in education.

This answer can be compared to the others that I discussed and criticized in earlier chapters. Unlike the views of theory and practice that characterize theory in special kinds of ways, as a scientific theory or as a normative theory, this view does not make theory into some special case that cannot be met in the case of teaching. My view only requires that the teacher have some knowledge base which is defined by the practice of teaching. It is, as I have made clear, a disparate lot; it may be that "lore" is the best description that we can provide for it. My position does not require that this knowledge base meet certain predetermined characteristics that would make it scientific or whatever.

The account of theory and practice that I offer does locate the deliberation about these issues in the teacher's practice. In that teachers must decide what they will do and how they will change their beliefs, it requires that the teacher be a "reflective practitioner," but it does not require that we create an alternative epistemology; it does not require that we make decisions about the nature of science and "technical rationality." It only requires that one subscribe to a small number of principles. These principles are consistent with any conception of science and practice that we might adopt. The problems that were encountered in examining a proposal for an alternative epistemology, one of reflection-in-action, are avoided while the strengths of that position remain.

Finally, this view is consistent with attempts to characterize teaching from the point of view of practice. Teaching on my account is still an intentional activity, but there is room in my account for a greater variety of knowledge that can be employed in teaching. The results of empirical research on teaching as well as the results of experience are part of the knowledge base that is employed by the teacher in making decisions about what to do.

There is a final test to which I would like to put my account of theory and practice. The issue of theory and practice arises in the context of teacher education. There we are concerned to provide prospective teachers with knowledge, or theory, that will result in professional, effective practice in the classroom. Another way in which my account can be justified is if it has something to say of importance and interest about the education of teachers. That will be my concern in the next chapter.

CHAPTER 8

Teacher education

The education of teachers is a topic of no small controversy. The problems of education and of our schools are often laid at the feet of those who prepare teachers; the solutions are often claimed to be found there as well. If we could only, the position goes, improve the preparation of teachers we could solve the problems to be found in our schools. The problems that face the schools and teacher education are diverse to say the least.[1] There are demographic issues; the number of people at the age typically associated with teacher education is diminishing in many Western countries while the demand for teachers is showing signs of increasing. There are economic issues; the changing economies in many countries are opening employment possibilities outside teaching for those who historically have been the main supply of candidates for the teaching profession. There are political issues; governments show a lack of consistency in their interest in the quality of education. It moves between high and low priority, leaving those involved in education confused about the importance to be assigned to their work. There are issues within higher education that impinge upon teacher education; the place and value that the study of education has in a university is not clear. Teacher education finds itself caught between the expectations of the profession it serves and the institutions which house it. What the teaching profession thinks is important for teacher education programs may not be what will gain them credibility within the universities that provide them homes. Teacher education is also affected by the problems and concerns of the practice of teaching; there is little reason to believe that teacher education can be made more successful if teaching itself cannot be made more attractive. These are but some of the issues that those involved in teacher education have been called upon to consider.

It is, thus, with trepidation that I enter the discussion of teacher education; there is so much that can be said. To provide a focus for my discussion, I will focus on the question: What is it that a person wanting to be a teacher needs to know? There is, to be sure, nothing modest about this question, but it does allow me to limit my discussion to that aspect of the problem which is most closely related to my concerns in these pages. By limiting the discussion in this way, I do not have to face the demographic, economic, political and administrative problems of teacher education, to name but a few. Also, I will not talk of teacher education in terms of courses and requirements. The exact form that a teacher education program will take is related to the context in which it occurs as well as to the compromises that have to be made in such contexts. Teacher education programs owe much to the history of their institutions and to the people who work in them. However, any attempt to think about teacher education will have to consider the general question that transcends institutional boundaries: What does a teacher need to know?

The complexity of teaching

There is one fact about teaching that needs to be discussed before I take on this general question. The impression may have been left from what I have said that teaching is, in a sense, a simple activity. By this I mean that teaching is an activity in which one selects an intention which will characterize the teaching situation and then one performs certain actions designed to realize the intention. Once, that is, a teacher has chosen that which students should learn no changes are required in the formulation of the teaching situation. What I have said in these pages is indeed compatible with teaching being a simple activity in this sense. But, my position is also compatible with teaching being a complex activity. That it is compatible in this way is a strength of this view because teaching often, if not always, is a complex activity. By a complex activity I mean one in which the situation affects and can change the original intention of the situation. That is, an activity in which the original intention cannot be carried through because the situation requires that the intention be modified is a complex activity. Such activities may also be called "interactive" in that the situation created by the teacher's original intention acts on that intention to change and modify it.

Let me first illustrate how teaching can be a complex activity. Suppose a teacher chooses as the original intention of a teaching situation that students should learn that the principles of the Hegelian dialectic are "thesis, antithesis and synthesis." The teacher puts these words on the chalk board before discussing them. The first question that is posed is by a student who wants to know who these three people are.[2] The teacher, here, has created an intentional situation in which the students have become participants. In asking the question, the student has revealed that he is willing to make the intention his own, but he has also revealed to the teacher, at least to the attentive teacher, that the original intention needs to be modified. The student's question shows that before the students can learn the principles of the Hegelian dialectic they need to learn the meaning of these three words. The original intention assumed that this meaning would be clear and that one could go on to explain how the three notions fit into the conception of dialectic. The teacher's interaction with the students in the teaching situation in this case should lead to a revision in the teacher's intention, and of course in the subsequent teaching. This shows one way in which teaching is complex; the student's lack of presumed knowledge can force the teacher to revise the intention to include other kinds of teaching so that the original intention can more likely be realized.

To show that this is not the only kind of revision to intentions that can take place in this interactive way, consider the teacher whose intention it is to teach a class that South Dakota is the only American state whose name has no letter in common with the name of its state capital.[3] In the course of the teacher's efforts to realize this intention the students make clear to the teacher that they find the point of this teaching to be absolutely trivial in that they can see no practical use for this information and in that they cannot see how the information could be fruitful as part of their general knowledge of the world. They, that is, demonstrate to the teacher that they have no interest in learning what the teacher intends for them to learn. The teacher's reaction may be to agree with the students and give up the original intention. This case shows that it is at least possible for the interaction with students to result in the original intention being dropped.

These cases show that teaching need not be a simple activity in which the teacher decides what students should learn and then goes about teaching what is required for the intention to be realized. Rather, teaching can be a complex activity in which the intention that created the teaching situation can be modified, expanded or even dropped during the course of the teaching. The final result of teaching may have little relation to the intention that started the teaching in the first place. How, it might be asked, is all this consistent with the view of teaching I have developed?

In my account of teaching, I argued that it is characterized by the intention of the teacher. This is what sets the intentional situation in which students come to participate with the teacher. The situation defines and provides the significance of the activity for both students and teachers. I have also provided an account of reasoned revision of intentions. I have argued that a central part of practical reasoning, which would be central to teaching practice, is the changes one makes to one's intentions. It is when these two strands of argument are seen together that teaching can be seen to be a complex activity. The intentions of teaching, like all intentions, are not immune from revision. When problems are encountered in teaching, they may lead to the revision of the teacher's beliefs or intentions. To teach the Hegelian dialectic to students who do not know the meaning of the words being used is to engage in a futile activity; the students will not learn what is being taught if they do not understand what the teacher is talking about. The Principle of Coherence would yield in this case that the teacher's intention to get students to learn about the Hegelian dialectic would be more coherent, in light of the discovery of the student's ignorance, if the teacher also intended that students learned the vocabulary used in this dialectic.

In my previous example of the instance where the names of a state and its capital share no common letters, the teacher dropped the intention as result of student opposition to the intention. This revision of intention is accounted for by the Principle of Desire Satisfaction. The teacher discovered in the course of teaching that the students had desires about their learning that were not in accord with the teacher's desire. In considering which desire was the more important, the teacher decided that it was his desire that needed to be revised. For the teacher's actions to cohere with this revised judgment of desirability, the original intention had to be revised. These examples show that the complexity of teaching (the interaction between the teacher's intentions and the events and circumstances of teaching) are actually a part of the practical reasoning that teachers engage in with respect to their intentions for the learning that students should acquire in the course of teaching.

Thus, the complexity that is a part of the teacher's life is consistent with the account of teaching and practical reasoning that I have provided. Indeed, it seems that this complexity can be accounted for by this account. As well, this complexity is a central fact of teaching, so that to learn to teach is to learn to deal with it. Part of what one needs to know to be a teacher, then, is to know how to revise one's intentions so that what is done is reasonable. This adds an important aspect to the education of teachers which is the general issue to which I will now turn.

What a teacher needs to know

With this discussion of the complexity of teaching and with my accounts of teaching and theory and practice in the previous chapters, the stage is now set for my account of teacher education, or, as I said earlier my focus would be, my answer to the question of what a teacher needs to know. Framing the question in this way indicates that my account of teacher education will be an outgrowth of what constitutes the practice of teaching. To enter the practice of teaching is to enter a community of sorts where one takes up the life of that community. To become a teacher is to enter into the ways of teaching. So, the practice of teaching sets the goals and agenda for teacher education. Putting the issue in this way is bound to raise certain objections that I wish to forestall.

One such objection is that if one takes the practice to be irremediably defective, one would oppose any form of teacher education that is an outgrowth of such a practice. The point of teacher education, here, would be to change practice, not to reproduce it. There is a bit of truth here; no approach to teacher education should, or probably can, reproduce current teaching practice exactly. This is not to say that teacher education should not be an outgrowth of teaching practice. The practice of teaching sets the parameters, as it were, for the activities of teaching. As teaching is characterized by the intention to bring about learning, the practice of teaching consists of the ways in which practitioners have attempted to realize that intention. These attempts are, of course, not always successful and some are probably misguided and inappropriate. This does not mean, though, that every such attempt is misguided. To say that teacher education should be an outgrowth of the practice of education is not, then, to commit one to continuing past mistakes. It is to say that teacher education should be concerned with passing on to prospective teachers what has been learned in the course of teaching practice that can contribute to the realization of the intention to bring about learning. So, even though we want to eradicate bad practice, there is no reason to avoid practice entirely when planning for the education of teachers.

A second objection might be that in making teacher education an outgrowth of teaching practice we would turn teaching into a routinized, non-reflective activity. The concern, here, is that if prospective teachers are taught to do what teachers in the field do, they will learn set behaviors that can be employed without having to think about whether they are appropriate or desirable. On the contrary, the objection continues, pro-spective teachers need to learn general theories and principles that will be utilized in intelligent and insightful ways. Again, to say that teacher education is an outgrowth of teaching practice is not to limit teacher education in the way this objection envisages. If teaching practice is itself an activity that requires intelligence and insight, as I hope to have established, then a teacher education program that is an outgrowth of teaching practice will be one that seeks to develop this intelligence and insight. So, the position that teacher education flows from teaching practice is not a position that necessarily results in teacher education being focused on routine behaviors that a teacher can perform.

If teacher education is an outgrowth of teaching practice, we can organize the discussion of teacher education by using the characteristics of teaching practice. One straightforward account is, "Competent teach-ing is a compound of three elements: subject matter knowledge, system-atic knowledge of teaching, and reflective practical experience."[4] I will consider these three elements as elements of teacher education.

Subject matter knowledge

I have discussed subject matter knowledge as one of the knowledge sources for the practice of teaching.[5] Before commenting on it from the point of view of teacher education, I need to make a few more comments on its place in teaching. I have argued that in the course of teaching one often finds oneself in the position of having to revise one's beliefs and intentions. In making such revisions in a reasonable way, one strives to make one's beliefs and intentions coherent. As part of the knowledge that a teacher brings to the teaching situation, subject matter knowledge needs to be coherent with the teacher's intention. The beliefs that one holds with respect to what one teaches must fit in with the purposes that one has with respect to what is to be taught as well as with what one believes about how it is to be taught to the particular students in the teaching situation. So the possession of subject matter knowledge is necessary for teaching in a number of ways. It is necessary for the establishment of the intention of the teaching situation; one cannot form the intention for students to learn something if one has no beliefs about what it is that students should learn. It is necessary for the practice of teaching; one cannot teach students without having something to teach to them. And it is necessary to the reasoned revision of belief and intention; one's revised beliefs and intentions must be coherent with one's other beliefs which, in teaching, will include subject matter knowledge.

That subject matter knowledge is necessary for teaching is, of course, not a novel point, but it is a point that matters. It matters in quite straightforward ways as when a teacher passes on beliefs that are simply wrong. If such teaching is successful, the result is, of course, that students leave the teaching situation with incorrect beliefs. The possession of ignorance is, I take it, undesirable. If the teacher holds beliefs that are contrary to acceptable and public evidence and justification, that is, if the teacher is mistaken and there is evidence available to the teacher to show the mistake, then the teacher is responsible for passing on incorrect beliefs. This is, I believe, clearly undesirable. There is another basis for passing on false beliefs where the teacher should not be held liable. A belief may be false even though at a particular time in history the evidence available to one would support the belief as being true. That our Sun has eight planets was supported by evidence until the discovery of Pluto. At such a time, a teacher passing on the belief that the Sun has eight planets could not be held at fault. The only kind of liability the teacher might incur in this case is if the teacher had taught the students in such a way that it would have been impossible for them to accept the evidence for the existence of Pluto and to change their beliefs when it was reasonable to do so. That is, a problem in teaching arises here only if the teaching is such that it prevents students from revising their beliefs when appropriate.

A second way in which the necessity of subject matter knowledge matters is in those cases where the teacher works from absence of knowledge, rather than error. The learning of students is frustrated when the teacher has no beliefs, right or wrong, about matters that are important for students to learn. Instead of teaching students the wrong beliefs, as is the case in working from error, the teacher simply remains silent on a matter of importance. Such instances would occur in a classroom discussion where a topic comes up on which the teacher has no knowledge that would allow him to pursue the discussion. In such cases, clearly, valuable teaching opportunities are lost.

A third way in which the necessity of subject matter matters can be seen in the experience of a student teacher. Working with third grade students on a lesson on weights, she had a variety of objects for students to handle and estimate their weight. Looking at the clock, she decided to revise her intentions in order to end the lesson on time. Her revision was to have only a limited number of students handle the objects, yet all were to estimate their weights. In analyzing the apparent failure of the lesson, we agreed that the problem stemmed from the fact that the subject matter concern for improving the students' abilities to estimate the weight of objects required them to hold the objects. This was, to put the matter in the language of this work, not coherent with the revised intention of the lesson. Her intention to get the lesson finished on time did not allow students to do what was necessary from the point of view of the subject being studied. So, the failure to take into account subject matter knowledge can have serious effects on the formation and revision of intentions in teaching practice.

Given the necessity of subject matter knowledge and the fact that the lack of such knowledge has important consequences for teaching, let me turn to the question of what role teacher education has in the providing of subject matter knowledge. The perspective, topic and approach of this work do place limits on what I can justifiably say on this matter. The subject matter knowledge that one needs for teaching, say, social studies to students in tenth grade is not something I can say. The most that I can do in this work is to provide a framework for teacher education, one that is consistent with the view of the relation between the knowledge one brings to the teaching situation, the "theory," and the decisions one makes in course of teaching, the "practice." The specific details of the actual knowledge that one should possess must be left to the careful discussion of experts and practitioners in the various subject areas. What I can do is to provide a general account of the importance of subject matter knowledge, which I have done, and to suggest the considerations that should to be invoked in any attempt to provide the detailed knowledge needed in a specific subject matter.

This account of theory and practice requires that teachers have a high level of subject matter knowledge. That some subject matter is logically required has already been established; my point here is that a high level of knowledge is needed for one to teach in the optimal or most desirable way. The reasons why teaching is enhanced by a high level of subject matter knowledge stem from my accounts of teaching and of theory and practice. First, my account of teaching establishes that the intention, and the related plan for teaching, sets the teaching situation for the teacher and students. The teacher's intention determines the situation for all involved in it. This intention is dependent on the knowledge sources the teacher brings to the teaching situation. The teacher needs to know what he or she intends for students to learn, in both senses of this crucially ambiguous claim. The teacher must, first, be aware of what it is that is intended for students to learn; the intention cannot be unconscious or unknown to the teacher. In the second interpretation of the claim, the teacher needs to know that what is being taught is the case. Not only does one need to be aware of what one is teaching, one also needs to know, or at least believe, that what one intends to teach is true, in the case of teaching information, theories, beliefs and the like; in the case of teaching skills, the teacher needs to know how to perform the skill. To fail in this is to lessen the value of one's teaching. It is, of course, logically possible to teach students that which one knows to be false. It would be an interesting exercise to try to teach students that the earth is flat. A particularly skillful person might be able to pull it off; this would seem to be a difficult challenge in that so many other beliefs the students might have would need to be altered. But such an attempt would seem to cheapen teaching. The value in teaching comes from, at least, enabling students to have an accurate view of their world. It is hard to see what service one is performing for students when what one teaches them is false.[6]

That teaching requires one to know what one is teaching and is enhanced if one believes or knows that what one is teaching is indeed the case shows that the more one knows the more one can teach. A high degree of subject matter knowledge, thus, broadens the range of intentions the teacher can try to realize. Simply put, the more the teacher knows the more help he or she can be in the students' learning, at least in that learning that is a result of formal teaching. To enhance the possible learning of students is, to be sure, a worthwhile pursuit. Students can learn on their own, indeed much of their learning occurs in just this way. This is, however, no reason to allow teachers to have a minimal degree of subject matter knowledge. The learning of students may well be achieved more efficiently and purposefully if it is the result of another's teaching. Having a high level of subject matter knowledge is supported in the first instance by being of benefit to the learning that students can acquire.

It is also of benefit with respect to the teacher's ability to revise intentions and beliefs in the course of teaching practice. As I have shown, teaching is a complex activity in that one's intentions will often need to be revised in light of the interactions the teacher has with students in the teaching situation. The more knowledge the teacher possesses about the subject the more alternatives will be open to the teacher in practice. When the situation requires that one's intention be revised, the teacher will need to find another intention that coheres with the circumstances of the situation and provides the minimal change from the previous intention. The more knowledge the teacher has the greater the range of revised intentions that can be entertained. A teacher with limited knowledge of an area will be limited in the sorts of things that he or she can teach about that area. Deeper knowledge allows the teacher to see more possible ways of getting the ideas and knowledge related to a topic across to the students. Having a high degree of knowledge is, thus, desirable in that it allows for more reasoned revision to one's intentions and beliefs in teaching practice.

As I have already mentioned, this is not the place to describe the particular knowledge a teacher needs for a given subject matter; this is an issue that must be left to those with expert knowledge in the particular areas. They will be able to identify the range and level of knowledge needed by a competent practitioner. This will encompass the appropriate knowledge within the subject matter itself and how it fits into the program of studies for students at differing levels of ability and experience. There are two general characteristics that any account of subject matter should meet. The first is that a teacher would need to possess a large range of facts or information about the material to be taught. The importance of basic, factual knowledge can be seen in a number of ways. It is, as it were, the stuff of teaching; no matter whether the teacher's intention is for students to acquire information, to learn some principle, or to develop some kind of feeling, the teacher needs to provide students with information that can be the basis on which the intention for teaching can be realized. One cannot learn a principle or develop a feeling without having some facts which the principle explains or which the feeling is about. As well, factual information is of potential use to students in that the information taught may at some point in the students' lives be something that can be employed. Also, factual information can be startling, and, so, can serve as the start of inquiry into other matters. The factual information of history can provide students with a sense of the development of their society.[7] The greater the amount of such knowledge that teachers acquire in their preparation, the more resources they have to draw upon in their work with students.

Encyclopedic knowledge alone is not enough; the second general characteristic that should be met by programs providing a high level of subject matter knowledge to teachers in preparation is that teachers need to know how the information fits together. This would include, in the first place, a knowledge of the general principles that govern the subject matter. In the sciences, for example, the teacher would need to know the theory or theories that link pieces of information and explain them. In music, one would need to know the aesthetic principles that justify the particular bits of information one provides when teaching students to play a musical instrument. We might call this the "structure" of the subject matter, as many have done, because such theories or sets of principles provide frameworks to which the facts or bits of information can be attached to provide a coherent whole.

A second way in which teachers need to see how a subject matter fits together is to know its methods of inquiry, what we might call its "logic." Every subject matter, or discipline, has ways in which it admits new claims as proven or acceptable and rejects other claims as unproven, wrong or unacceptable. In some cases, the methods are relatively straightforward. The use of experiment in the sciences and deduction in mathematics are such cases. In spite of any difficulties in understanding these methods, they are the basic ways by which one determines what claims are to be accepted or rejected in these disciplines. In other areas, the methods of inquiry are much less clear or even fundamentally at dispute. But, there is some logic to them all, it would seem. Not any interpretation of a poem is acceptable, not any collection of sound is music, not any arrangement of color on a canvas is art. We may not be able to state the methods that are used, but teachers need to have a feel or awareness of what within their teaching area can be accepted and what must be rejected.[8]

Finally, a teacher needs to have an awareness of what we might call the "philosophy" of the subject in order to see how it fits together. By this I mean the teacher should see the relation of this subject matter to others. To put the point roughly, the teacher should see the place of the subject matter in the larger scheme of things. (This also shows that I am using "philosophy" here in a very loose sense.) The science teacher not only needs to know the facts of science, the theories of science and the methods of science, she needs to know the place of science in one's culture. This would require some knowledge of the history of science, how it came to be, and of the sociology of science, its place as a social institution in our world. The teacher would need to know how scientific insight is different from poetic or religious insight. One should also have some awareness of the moral issues that can be raised by the practice of science. The teacher needs to be able to pass on to students not just the detail of a subject but to provide students with ways of relating that subject to others.

This last point on the way in which the teacher needs to have knowledge of how the subject matter fits together leads, in a way, to my final point about subject matter knowledge. In making the point I will apparently extend the meaning of "subject matter" quite far, beyond the breaking point some will no doubt say. My concern, here, is the general knowledge that the teacher possesses, the knowledge one has that goes beyond the limits of any particular subject area or discipline. I include this in my discussion of subject matter knowledge, because, the intrinsic value of being an educated person notwithstanding, every teacher is a teacher of general knowledge. Even at levels of education where teachers are assigned to teach particular subjects, as in our secondary schools and universities, teachers need to draw upon knowledge from outside their assigned teaching areas. Their original intention for the teaching situation may be based entirely in their subject, but it may have to be revised as a result of interaction with students to include discussion of topics that relate to the original topic but which may belong to another realm of thought. For example, a chemistry curriculum in use in my local schools includes material that deals with the extraction of oil from bitumen; it tries to develop general knowledge of chemistry in the context of an industry that is common knowledge among students in this part of the world. Chemistry teachers using this curriculum will inevitably find themselves discussing the economic and political issues that attend this chemical process. To the extent that we as a society want to promote general education amongst those who attend our schools, teachers, no matter how narrow their assigned teaching area, need to be models of educated persons for their students.

Professional knowledge

The second area of teacher education I wish to discuss is the systematic knowledge of teaching, what I will call for short "professional knowledge." I include two aspects of this knowledge: the first is the knowledge a person needs of the casual laws, regularities, or relations that may produce learning; the second is the knowledge a person needs about teaching, that is, of the place of teaching in our social and educational concerns. Of the three areas I will discuss, this would seem to be the most controversial. No one claims, at least to my knowledge, that a person can be prepared to be a teacher without subject matter knowledge and the opportunity for reflective, practical experience. Many claim, on the other hand, that one does not need systematic knowledge of teaching in order to be a teacher; one just needs subject matter knowledge and the opportunity for practice, the rest will come with time. I need first of all to defend my inclusion of providing systematic knowledge of teaching as a part of teacher education.

The inclusion of this knowledge in teacher education cannot be defended on the grounds of necessity. There are too many examples of people who have been successful as teachers who have never had any instruction in the systematic knowledge of teaching. It is simply contrary to fact to say that it is impossible to teach without being introduced to the systematic knowledge of teaching. My defense of its inclusion in teacher education will, then, be on the grounds of its desirability rather than on its necessity.

The first step in this argument is to notice that although it is true that it is possible to teach without having acquired professional knowledge in a teacher education program, it does not follow that it is possible to teach without having professional knowledge. I want to argue that professional knowledge is required for teaching and, further, that of all the ways one can acquire this knowledge, its inclusion in a teacher education program is the most desirable. One can acquire this knowledge in a variety of ways, but one must acquire it in some way. My point is that the best way to acquire it is to have it included, or at least have the basis for it laid, in teacher education programs.

I need to make two points: the first is that professional knowledge is required for teaching. This point is implied by my account of teaching. One result of teaching being an intentional activity is that the teacher must have a plan for realizing the intention. If a person claimed to intend A but had no idea or plan for bringing A about, we would deny that the person intends A. That is, a person cannot have an intention without some sort of plan to bring it about. As pointed out earlier, the plan may be sketchy, but it must be there. In teaching, where the intention is to bring about some learning, the plan will involve steps that one can take that, at least in one's view, will make it more likely that learning will result. The steps will be actions that one, as a teacher, can perform that will be a causal factor in learning. One of the components of professional knowledge, systematic knowledge of teaching, is the causal knowledge of what actions result in learning. So, to engage in teaching logically requires that one have some beliefs about what would count as professional knowledge. This is a logical result of teaching being an intentional activity. So, the first point is established, albeit in a somewhat weaker form than originally stated; it is necessary that a teacher have some beliefs about professional knowledge.

My second point, that it is desirable to include professional knowledge in teacher education programs, will be in two parts. The first is that it is better to have systematic knowledge of teaching than some beliefs about what would count as such knowledge. The second is that it is better to include this knowledge in teacher education programs than to leave it to alternative sources. My support for the first point is similar to the support I provided earlier for the claim that teacher education should provide prospective teachers with a high degree of subject matter knowledge. Imagine two teachers; one with some beliefs about what actions will cause learning, all that is logically required for teaching, and another with systematic knowledge of teaching. I want to claim that the second person is the better prepared for teaching. One way to see this point is to look at the teacher as practical reasoner. Teachers will often be engaged in the activity of revising their intentions. When an intention is revised one needs to hold up the revised intention against one's beliefs to determine if the proposed revision is coherent with what one believes. If one has only a limited number of beliefs that relate to possible plans of action, then the number of possible revised intentions that will be coherent with one's beliefs will be limited. The greater the number of beliefs one has the greater the range of revised intentions one can entertain. Further, if one has knowledge of teaching, rather than just beliefs, the likelihood that one's revised intentions will be coherent with actual states of affairs is increased. So, having systematic knowledge of teaching provides the teacher with a greater range of possible intentions one can utilize in the revisions of one's intentions for teaching. Having picked up through experience, to use an artificial example, two techniques for presenting material to learning disabled children provides a teacher with less room for maneuver than if one had learned five techniques in a teacher preparation program. Having a greater range of possible intentions makes the teacher more prepared for dealing with teaching situations. Being more prepared, I submit, can make it more likely that the teacher will be successful. If it can make the teacher more successful, then, the teacher is better prepared for the task of teaching. This establishes that having systematic professional knowledge is better than some beliefs about what brings about learning.

This point rests on two assumptions that I have not considered. The first is that, as a matter of fact, educational research and our study of teaching provide more systematic knowledge of teaching than one can reasonably pick up through experience. I shall not defend this assumption except to point out that the progress in educational research and research on teaching in recent years makes it likely that the body of systematic knowledge we have on teaching is greater than what one can learn through personal experience, at least for the beginning teacher. The second assumption is that the systematic knowledge that one has will be used. If the teacher possesses systematic knowledge in the back of one's mind, as it were, and does not call upon it in the course of revising one's intentions, then there is no benefit to having the knowledge. This suggests that the learning of this knowledge should occur in such a way as to make the knowledge as "lively" as possible for the teacher, that is, so that it is likely to be utilized. This leads to my second point on the desirability of including professional knowledge in teacher education.

In my defense of including professional knowledge in teacher education, I have established that some beliefs about the causal regularities of teaching are necessary and that systematic knowledge of teaching is more desirable than having some beliefs; I now need to show that it is better to learn this knowledge in a teacher education program than in any other way. John Passmore identifies seven ways in which we derive information: observation, from experience, through experience, what we pick up from others, what we learn by study, what we infer from other information and what is imparted to us by a teacher.[9] Of these ways of acquiring information of the systematic knowledge of teaching, having a teacher impart it is the most efficient. A teacher, at least a good one, will be able to organize this knowledge so that it can be acquired with the least difficulty. Dead ends and unproductive lines of inquiry can be prevented. Material from varieties of sources can be brought together and synthesized by the teacher. A person familiar with the knowledge will be able to answer questions and suggest further lines of inquiry. All this suggests that much time will be saved if this knowledge is imparted to us by a teacher. This is not to say that the knowledge cannot be acquired in other ways; surely one could obtain this knowledge through independent study. My point is that it will be obtained more efficiently and systematically if it is learned from a teacher. I conclude, then, that professional knowledge is justified as a part of teacher education because it is both needed and most efficiently learned when it is imparted by a teacher.

Reflective practical experience

The third component of teacher education is reflective practical experience. Practical experience has always been a part of teacher education programs, usually in the form of student teaching, although it can be provided for in a variety of ways. My concern is that this experience be reflective as well. To establish this point I need to clarify the terms of the discussion, provide reasons for the inclusion of practical experience in teacher education and, finally, demonstrate the merits of reflective practical experience. I will begin by considering only practical experience.

The range of what might be meant by "practical experience" is so great that for purposes of this discussion I will need to be more precise. After all, to sit and listen to a lecture is as much an experience as teaching thirty third grade children. Our ordinary understanding of experience, that is, does not do much to differentiate what is at issue, here, from subject matter or professional knowledge. The notion of being practical in its ordinary usage does not add much either. Whether something is practical depends on the purposes of the person having the experience. A person attending a lecture may find it of great practical use because the content of the lecture gives her information needed in her own work, while another person attending the same lecture may find it of no practical use because, although he thoroughly enjoys the lecture, its content is unrelated to any of his current projects. To focus the discussion, let me offer the following as a characterization of practical experience. Those opportunities and occasions that are provided to intending teachers to try out or test their ideas and to practice the skills they have learned or been taught will be the instances of what I mean by practical experience. This separates practical experience from the learning of subject matter and professional knowledge which can be acquired in relatively passive situations even though such learning may be of great practical benefit to the intending teacher. It focuses on what can be learned when one tries to put this knowledge into practice.

Practical experience is an essential part of teacher education. In teacher education our concern is not just with the possession of knowledge; we are concerned as well with the utilization of knowledge. The outcome of teacher education is intended to be the ability to teach, not just knowledge about teaching. That teacher education is intended to result in people having the ability to teach makes practical experience essential. It is probably not inconceivable or incoherent to imagine that a person could learn how to teach without having had practical experience. It is not logically impossible to conceive of a person receiving instruction in subject matter and professional knowledge and, then, starting to teach in a competent manner. This does strike one as highly unlikely, which is to say that practical experience is essential but not logically so. It is essential in that to learn to perform as a teacher requires practice to refine one's abilities. Through practice one becomes more aware of what one is doing and increases the knowledge one has of the skill one is performing.[10] Practice may be blind repetition but it need not be. When it is not, it is done for a particular point. One may practice one's questioning techniques in order to improve one's ability to ask questions that require students to analyze rather than to remember, or one may practice questioning in order to become better at providing students with time to think about the answer to the question. When one practices for a particular point, one becomes more aware of what is happening with respect to that skill in the particular case and one may gain knowledge about the skill from the practice. The knowledge that one becomes aware of through practice can be of a different sort than that learned in other contexts. One difference is that knowledge acquired in practice will be specific to the context. What one learns in practice, that this questioning format is more effective than that, will always be specific to that context in which it was learned. One discovers, that is, that this questioning technique is more effective than that for this group of children studying this topic on this occasion. There is nothing about the practice that suggests that the discovery would necessarily be generalizable to other situations. In practical situations, one is concerned to discover what is true for the situation at hand, not what is true in general. So, one's interest is in specific knowledge. This, of course, is in contrast with the interests involved in subject matter and professional knowledge where the concern is for what is generally true.

It is through practical experience that one acquires specific knowledge with respect to particular groups of children learning certain subjects. This is knowledge the teacher must have; it is the knowledge that comes as one tries to utilize the subject matter and professional knowledge that one may have. Without practical experience, the teacher's knowledge can remain knowledge about teaching. With practical experience, the teacher acquires a different kind of knowledge, context-specific knowledge, that helps to further one's ability to utilize the knowledge that one brings to the teaching situation. Practical experience is essential in this sense for providing the teacher with the opportunity to acquire knowledge in teaching, rather than just to have knowledge about teaching.

I want to claim that more than practical experience is needed for teaching, the practical experience should be reflective as well. To give a sense to this notion, let me begin with the fact that one acquires knowledge in practical experience. This knowledge is, as I have said, specific to a context. When a teacher finds herself in a different context where it is not clear whether the knowledge from the first context will hold, she has two options. One, she may have reason to believe that the knowledge does not hold, in which case she has to revise her beliefs for the new context. Two, she may think the knowledge from the first context does hold or she may have no idea whether it holds in the second. In this case, she will act as if it does, in which case the knowledge may or may not hold. If not, the teacher again has to revise her beliefs. So, in either case, the need for the revision of one's beliefs becomes a possibility. I will call practical experience that results in a teacher having to revise his or her beliefs reflective practical experience. In these terms, practical experience becomes reflective when the practitioner engages in the revision of intentions and beliefs.

That the practical experience of the intending teacher be reflective is important for the following reason. First, it is important because the teacher needs to learn how to adapt to differing contexts. The knowledge one gains in practical experience is specific to that context, but one will find oneself teaching in a variety of contexts. Since what is learned in one context need not be generalizable to other contexts, the teacher will need to make adjustments to what is learned. What is learned in one context often cannot be applied in other contexts without some revisions to one's beliefs. The intending teacher needs to learn how to make such revisions in order that application of one's knowledge to different circumstances is appropriate. In providing practical experiences that require reflection to intending teachers, we provide them the opportunity to learn how to revise beliefs and intentions. The need to revise beliefs and intentions is one that is, perhaps, inevitable in teaching.

To provide intending teachers with reflective practical experiences in this sense requires more than to place people with subject matter and professional knowledge in teaching situations. In the first place, not all experiences require reflection. If someone is in a situation where previous learnings will suffice without revision, one need not reflect on the situation. If one's practical experience is limited to the teaching of one topic to one group of children or to several groups of very similar children, one may not have to revise one's beliefs or intentions. In order to insure that the intending teacher has the opportunity for reflective practical experience, it would seem that a range of experiences should be provided so as to increase the likelihood that the person will have practical experiences that require reflection, that is ones that will put the intending teacher in the position of having to revise his or her beliefs and intentions.

This, though, is not enough. It is one thing to provide people with the opportunity to have reflective practical experience, it is something else to enable them to profit from those experiences. As I have tried to detail, practical reasoning, the kind that occurs in reflective practical experiences, has a logic. One can be prepared to be a practical reasoner. If one is to profit from reflective practical experiences, one should have the abilities required to revise one's beliefs and intentions in reasonable ways. The specifics of what one needs to know to revise beliefs and intentions will vary between subject areas and between age levels and, so, are not the concern of this work, but some general points can be made.

The first principle that governs the reasoned change of beliefs and intentions is the Principle of Coherence. A number of general abilities are involved in the application of this principle that can be learned. One who has learned these abilities will be in a better position to profit from reflective practical experiences than one who has not. The basic interest that anyone has in seeking coherence is to avoid inconsistencies. To learn to recognize inconsistencies and contradictions will, thus, enable one to meet this interest. This ability can, of course, be learned in a variety of ways; the way that is chosen is of no great matter so long as this elementary feature of critical thought is learned at some point in the teacher's preparation. The coherence that obtains among a person's beliefs will be given in relations of implication and explanation. This, too, suggests important elements in the preparation of teachers. They need to learn at some point the relations of implication so that they can see when beliefs are validly related and when beliefs that are putatively related are, in fact, fallaciously related. They need as well to be able to identify satisfactory explanations. This ability is, to be sure, complex. Part of this ability stems from the person's knowledge of the subject. One needs to know the facts and theories of an area in order to tell if explanations within the area are coherent. This would seem to be necessary but not sufficient. Encyclopedic knowledge of an area would not seem to guarantee an ability to discern satisfactory and unsatisfactory explanations. One needs as well to have an understanding of the principles of explanation as they relate to the subject matter. Finally, the Principle of Coherence requires that one's explanations not be based on false assumptions. The ability to locate the assumptions on which a position rests is something one can learn.

In the revision of intentions, one also has to appeal to the Principle of Desire Satisfaction. For a person to be reflective in practical experience, then, one has at least to be able to identify and order one's own desires. When intentions have conflicting ends, the practitioner needs to be able to decide which is the more important. This suggests that one should, as part of one's preparation for practical experience, learn a range of possible desires that can be appealed to in teaching and learn to evaluate possible candidates for what should be desired. The education of children should not be limited to the desires that the person happens to bring to teacher preparation. Teachers need to learn the range of possible desires that may be appealed to in teaching and to evaluate these candidates so that the students are best served.

An outline of a teacher education program

To draw the points of this discussion together, I would like to present one way in which teacher education could be organized. In doing so, I will claim nothing that is radical or extreme. Although contemporary teacher education programs contain the general elements of what is called for by the arguments I have presented, there are certain aspects of what I see as demanded by my general conception of teacher education that are not given sufficient attention. I also make no claim that this outline is the only outline for teacher education. There are, no doubt, other outlines that could be constructed that would be consistent with my general position. The outline I have chosen is meant to be consistent with current organizational structures in universities as well as with my general positions on teaching and teacher education. For example, I am taking for granted that the knowledge intending teachers need will be organized into course offerings taught by university instructors who meet the qualifications and expectations of universities, that many of the practical experiences intending teachers have will be in schools, or school-like institutions, under the general control of universities, at least in the sense that universities rather than schools will certify successful completion of these experiences, and that intending teachers will have to meet the admission requirements that universities may set. All of these factors, and others not mentioned, probably deserve to be questioned. To do so could result in radically different teacher education programs. I take a more sanguine view: it is difficult enough to change teacher education programs; to change both teacher education programs and the ways universities go about organizing themselves is to approach the impossible.

I will use the three components of teacher education from the last section to organize this outline. The first is subject matter knowledge. Under this, it will be remembered, I have included the general knowledge that a teacher needs. A teacher education program needs to include a strong program of general education. Regardless of the subjects they intend to teach or the age levels of the students with whom they will work, teachers need to be broadly and generally educated. Whatever else teachers are, they are models for their students. If we take seriously that students should leave schools as educated persons, however we might flesh out this concept, we must expect teachers themselves to be such persons. If teachers are not expected to be educated persons, it is unlikely that students will become so. I leave open the details and arrangements for the general education program for teachers; institutions with their histories and policies will have to work out for themselves what it means to be educated and how this can be achieved. There is one danger I would point out. Too often in education, particularly higher education, we see courses as preparation for the next course in a sequence. A course is developed in the interest of those students following the sequence when in fact many if not most of the students in the course will not follow the sequence. A department of economics may see its general introductory course as providing the basis for advanced work in economics when in fact the vast majority of students in the course will never take another course in economics. In terms of general education, we should conceive courses as the last course students will take in the field rather than the first. In this case, an economics course in general education should be concerned with what an educated citizen should know about economics, not with what a prospective economics major needs to know in order to profit from later courses in economics.

With respect to knowledge of the particular subject area or areas that the prospective teacher will teach, this outline cannot, of course, give the details for each and every possible area. These will have to be provided by the experts in the areas. Programs that provide prospective teachers with sufficiently deep and complete knowledge of what they will be teaching will have to be devised for all teaching areas. There is an immense practical difficulty, here, given the differences between the ways universities organize themselves and the ways in which schools assign teachers to their duties. The teacher of young children is expected to teach all, or at least a wide range of, subjects while universities compartmentalize subjects in ways foreign to the teacher's work. Even in the higher grades, where the curriculum is organized in ways more similar to the organization in universities, teachers are given assignments that can include a number of distinct subjects. Ways of articulating the development of subject matter knowledge in universities with the responsibilities of teachers in schools need to be examined.

There is one general issue concerning subject matter knowledge that must be recognized. The subject matter knowledge of a teacher has to be different in important respects from that of one pursuing the subject on its own. That is, what a biology teacher needs to know is different from what a biologist needs to know. The difference is at what might be called the "meta-level." Both biologists and biology teachers need to know biology in its depth and breadth; ideally a biology teacher and a biologist would be equally competent. The teacher, though, needs a kind of knowledge of the subject matter that the biologist does not. The teacher needs to understand the subject in its relation to other subjects and as part of the overall education of students. The biology teacher, for example, not only must master biology but must also be able to see and explain biology as an area of knowledge that is important for students. She should be able to understand how biology fits with the other subjects the students are learning, how it can be justified as part of the education of a person not pursuing biology for practical reasons and how biology is similar to and different from other approaches to studying the world. None of these concerns must be met in the practice of biology itself, although one hopes that biologists would be sensitive to these questions, but they must be faced in the teaching of biology. So, teachers need this kind of awareness of their subject that is over and above the actual content of the subject.[11]

The professional knowledge component of my outline for teacher education falls into two parts. The first part of professional knowledge about teaching relates to my claim that teaching is a causal process or, in other words, that the relations between teaching activities and the bringing about of learning are causal relations. A teacher education program must provide prospective teachers with this causal knowledge. The results of educational research that provide us with an understanding of the relation between the actions of teachers and their effects on students will be at the core of professional knowledge in teacher education. Along with this there is much else that can be provided such as a general understanding of the psychology of students and of the curriculum that is presented to students. Each of these get their focus from the causal relations of teaching. Psychology that does not concern itself with what teachers do to bring about changes in students is not educational psychology. The study of curriculum that does not look at what teachers do to bring about the learning intended by the curriculum is an academic, in the pejorative sense of the term, study at best. The account of teaching I have proposed allows a wide range of material that can be taught to prospective teachers, but it requires that an understanding of the causal relations in teaching be presented.

The second aspect of professional knowledge that is included in my outline stems from the Principle of Desire Satisfaction that is used in reasoned change in view. This principle states that in changing one's intentions one should select the intention that satisfies one's desires. As pointed out in the last section, this requires that one be aware of one's desires and that one's range of desires be expanded. In my outline of a teacher education program, this means that room must be made for the development of these issues. There would seem to be three specific areas that should be included. First, prospective teachers need the skills to evaluate desires. They should come to understand the nature of desires in the context of education and what principles might be used in deciding which desires are worth pursuing. Second, they need to be introduced to a range of purposes and desires that can be held for education. By studying various proposals for the aims and content of education, prospective teachers can come to see that their original concerns and desires are not the only possible ones that can be pursued. It seems to me that these two areas are best approached together; the range of possible desires that can be presented would provide the context in which evaluation skills could be developed. The third area, here, is an understanding of the social context in which desires are satisfied. A sociological understanding of the institution of education will help prospective teachers see the limits that might have to be placed on desire satisfaction. Issues of race, class, gender and ethnicity, for example, speak to the concerns society has for education. An historical understanding of schools will contribute to the prospective teacher's knowledge of how to use the Principle of Desire Satisfaction through learning of past experience of the ability of schools to achieve their purposes. That philosophy of education is central to the development of the Principle of Desire Satisfaction goes, I hope, without saying.

The final element in the outline for a teacher education program is reflective practical experience. Programs for the preparation of teachers have long been successful in providing practical experience for their students; my concern is that these experiences be reflective as well. The position on practical reasoning that I have advocated gives, as I have tried to make clear, a way of understanding the relation between theory and practice or, in simpler terms, between what we believe and what we do. Reflective practical experience is that in which one is called upon to revise one's intended actions in light of one's beliefs. Another virtue of this position is that, in providing a logic for reasoned change in view, it enables one to be prepared to be reflective in practice. Relating theory to practice, that is, is not something that we can only hope will happen during the course of a person's teacher education program or teaching career. It is something for which the basis can be taught. Intending teachers can be taught how to be reflective.

As the previous section has shown, the subject matter and professional knowledge that is included in a teacher education program is part of the preparation for reflective practical experience. The beliefs that the student acquires as a result of instruction in these areas provide the range of beliefs that will be utilized in experience. Proposed beliefs will, in the first instance, be held up and compared to the beliefs developed in teacher preparation. New ideas, that is, will be examined to see if they are coherent with those ideas the teacher brings to the situation. So, the beliefs and knowledge from teacher education will be at the basis of the teacher's use of the Principle of Coherence. This is, of course, not to say that these beliefs will survive all challenges. The result of experience and the use of the Principle of Coherence may well be, and likely will be, the dropping of some beliefs from teacher education in favor of some new beliefs. But, the initial store of beliefs will come from teacher education; so with a large number of sound beliefs the beginning teacher should be able to use the Principle of Coherence to advantage.

Another element of reflective practical experience for which intending teachers can be prepared prior to actual experience is the logical and critical skills that are necessary for reasoned change of belief and intention. Again, as seen in the previous section, the application of the Principles of Reasoned Change of Belief and Intention presuppose the ability to identify inconsistencies, relations of implication, assumptions and explanatory relations. These abilities can be taught to people, so, they can be taught to prospective teachers prior to practical experience. If they come to practical experience with these abilities, they are in a much better position to be reflective about that experience. That these abilities can be taught is, I think, clear; how we best organize the teaching of those skills is an empirical question whose answer is not, to my knowledge, clear. There are a range of possibilities. One, we can isolate these skills and teach them independently of other content in, say, a logic or informal logic course. Two, we can teach these abilities in the context of another course in the hope that they will be applied in practical experience. The abilities to recognize inconsistencies and to evaluate explanations can be developed in a science course or in a literature course. Whether learning these abilities in such contexts results in people being able to recognize inconsistencies and to evaluate explanations in practical experience is not clear, but it is a possibility that can be investigated. Finally, we can teach these abilities in conjunction with practical experience rather than prior to it. One can work with students who are engaged in practical experience in order to develop these abilities. For example, one can discuss the situation with students in such a way that inconsistencies are highlighted, that alternative explanations are proposed, that implications are pointed out. This can, if done well, result through further discussion and instruction in the student's acquisition of the skills required for reasoned change in view.

Subject matter and professional knowledge and the critical skills just discussed are the background knowledge for reflective practical experience. Let me now turn to the question of how the practical experience provided to intending teachers can help them to be reflective. Thinking of practical experience in this way gives it a special purpose and so organizes our thinking in particular ways. The purpose of practical experience is not to demonstrate competence as a teacher; it is not to give the student the chance to show that certain teaching skills have been mastered; it is not to show that the student can manage a classroom. Its point is to enable the student to develop the capacity for reasoned change in belief and intention, a capacity which I have argued throughout as being central to the practice of teaching. When we think of practical experience as being reflective in this way, our organization of these experiences for intending teachers may have to change.

This view of practical experience would require us, I think, to see what we call student teaching as a laboratory experience. To view practical experience under this description makes it clear that the point of such experience is to try out ideas. In a laboratory, one tests hypotheses, observes the outcomes and makes appropriate changes to one's beliefs — to put a highly complex activity in overly simplistic language. In such situations, the cases that are most helpful to becoming reflective are those where the hypothesis fails. In such cases the student sees that her belief was wrong and that a change in belief is necessary; the student is forced into practical reasoning. We learn little if our hypotheses are continually confirmed. A feature of many current student teaching programs is that students are not rewarded for mistakes; they can be under intense pressure to do what is safe and expected. The result is that learning to be reflective is inhibited. Taking practical experience to be a kind of laboratory will allow us to let students be more adventurous in testing out their ideas and to run the risk of failure. More will be learned about teaching when one's own ideas do not work and have to be rethought than when one repeats safe and conventional strategies.

Viewing practical experience as a kind of laboratory experience also requires us to view the supervisor in a special way. Schön suggests that in practical experience the supervisor needs to be a coach. "The student cannot be *taught* what he needs to know, but be can be *coached*."[12] He then quotes Dewey: "He has to *see* on his own behalf and in his own way the relations between means and methods employed and results achieved. Nobody else can see for him, and he can't see just by being 'told,' although the right kind of telling may guide his seeing and, thus, help him to see what he needs to see."[13] Schön is clearly identifying teaching with telling, an identification which is false and diminishes the plausibility of the claim. Telling is only one kind of teaching, it cannot be identified with teaching. If we restate the claim to be that the student cannot be told what he needs to know but he can be coached, there is much more plausibility. The supervisor of the intending teacher in the laboratory type of practical experience will not tell the intending teacher what he or she should do. Rather, the supervisor will observe the intending teacher, make criticisms, provide pointers, suggest alternatives, ask questions, give moral or psychological support, keep motivation alive and the like. This list of behaviors corresponds much more to the activities of a coach than to those of a lecturer. The supervisor will allow the intending teacher to test ideas and will serve as the evaluator of those ideas. In the course of this interaction with the intending teacher, the supervisor may be successful in enabling the intending teacher to become a reflective professional in teaching.

One way to promote this laboratory kind of experience is to structure the practical experience of intending teachers. It could begin with simulated and small group experiences that are independent of school settings. Beginning in this way, the intending teacher will not, it is to be hoped, see that taking risks is something to be avoided. By removing the pressure of school-based teaching from the practical experience, the student may be more willing to test beliefs in ways that are most challenging to those beliefs and are most beneficial to his or her learning. From there the intending teacher could move to more traditional student teaching experiences. This would involve limited teaching in a school under the relatively close supervision of the classroom teacher. This person would see himself as a coach who would provide for increasingly complex and independent teaching experiences for the intending teacher. Finally, the intending teacher could participate in an internship where he or she would work quite independently with a class for an extended period of time. Here, the supervisor or coach would be available for assistance and evaluation but would have much less regular contact with the intending teacher than would be the case in the student teaching stage of practical experience. Throughout, the emphasis would be on the development of reflective experiences, the kind the intending teacher will be responsible for as a professional teacher.

The Holmes Report

This account of theory and practice in teacher education, if it is to be helpful, should give us a way of probing and evaluating proposals for the reform of teacher education. It is this test to which I want to put my account. A particularly important reform of teacher education is given in the report of the Holmes Group, *Tomorrow's Teachers*.[14] The scope of this report is, to be sure, much greater than that attempted here. My concern has been to investigate a specific aspect of teacher education: how teachers relate their knowledge and beliefs to their decisions about what to do in classrooms. I have argued that a wide range of knowledge is necessary for making these decisions, but even so my attention has been focused on a narrower concern than is found in general reports on teacher education such as the Holmes Report. Because their range of interests is greater then mine, much of what they have to say will neither be supported nor criticized by my account. The position here, though, will speak to some areas of their concern.

The general position of the Holmes Report is captured by a quotation from Henry Holmes, the dean of the Harvard Graduate School of Education in the 1920s, from whom this group takes its name; schools of education need to prepare teachers who have, "the power of critical analysis in a mind broadly and deeply informed."[15] That this says little is apparent, but it is also apparent that what I have said is consistent with this. The more interesting question is whether the detail that the report provides to bring this power of critical analysis about fits with the position I have tried to defend. The reform of teacher education, according to the Holmes Group, must take into account, "the rewards and career opportunities for teachers; the standards, nature, and substance of professional education; the quality and coherence of the liberal arts and subject matter fields; and the professional certification and licensing apparatus."[16] Of these four areas, the first and fourth have been, perhaps, the most controversial aspects of the report. It is here that they develop a tripartite division of the teaching profession consisting of instructors, professional teachers and career professionals. They spell out the requirements for these classifications and discuss how one can be judged to be competent within these areas. Such considerations take them into discussions of the demand for teachers and the problems relating to the assignment of credentials. My position grows out of my account of teaching which would be common to all teachers regardless of professional label or ranking. As a result, my account is neutral with respect to the question of how the profession of teaching is organized and how individuals are licensed to participate in the profession. The position I have developed does not enable us either to criticize or support this aspect of the Holmes Report, so on this issue I shall remain silent.

Like the Holmes Report, I have discussed the importance of general and subject matter knowledge. In my account, they figure prominently as the background knowledge a teacher must possess in order to engage in practical reasoning. The Holmes Group provides three recommendations for the improvement of academic preparation:

> to sharply revise undergraduate curriculum so that future teachers can study the subjects they will teach with instructors who model fine teaching and who understand the pedagogy of their material, . . . to organize academic course requirements so that undergraduate students can gain a sense of the intellectual structure and boundaries of their disciplines, rather than taking a series of disjointed, prematurely specialized fragments, . . . [and] to devise coherent programs that will support the advanced studies in pedagogy required for solid professional education.[17]

In general, "teachers should know their subjects thoroughly and have the qualities of educated, thoughtful, and well-informed individuals."[18] These quotations indicate that the concern for general and subject matter knowledge is similar to mine. For them, it is essential to teaching in general; for me, it is part of the knowledge base of teaching that is utilized, among other things, in the teacher's practical reasoning. One must not only know one's subject thoroughly, one must use it in making decisions about what and how to teach. So, if my position is correct on this point, it lends support to the recommendations of the Holmes Group on this matter.

It is the Holmes Group's recommendations and discussion of professional knowledge that perhaps comes closest to my discussion. In discussing their view of teaching they say, "central to the vision are competent teachers empowered to make principled judgments and decisions on their students' behalf."[19] Their concerns about field experiences in teacher education programs echo mine.

> Rarely does the experience build upon the general principles and theories emphasized in earlier university study. . . .Most student teachers quickly conform to the practices of their supervising teacher and rarely put into practice a novel technique or risk failure. . . .The emphasis is on imitation of and subservience to the supervising teacher, not upon investigation, reflection, and solving novel problems.[20]

They cite as an alternative to traditional sites of student teaching the Professional Development School, which would be the analog of the teaching hospital. Among the advantages of such schools, they note the development of professional knowledge and practice. Such schools would, "provide an opportunity to test different instructional arrangements, under different types of working conditions."[21] The views I have put forward are not only consistent with these claims, they provide substance to these ideas which is not provided by the Holmes Report. I have tried to spell out in some detail what it means to be reflective as a teacher. It is, I would suggest, not enough to say that teachers should be reflective. We need to try to understand what a person needs to know and to be able to do in order to be a reflective teacher. In discussing the logic of such a notion in the context of how theory can be related to practice, the position I have developed is a useful addition, if not corrective, to the Holmes Report.

These comments are certainly not sufficient to endorse or reject the Holmes Report; that has not been their intention. All that I have claimed is that my position is consistent with a major report on teacher education and that it provides substance and direction to some of their recommendations. By showing this, it is also shown that my position not only fits in contemporary thought in teacher education, it provides as well an important supplement to these discussions by providing specific direction and substance to our thinking about how to reform teacher education.

Conclusion

The challenge in teacher education is to enable prospective teachers to take what they have learned about teaching and to use it on their own in the teaching situations in which they find themselves or, to put this in the terms of this work, to engage in practical reasoning as teachers. Teachers must form intentions based on their beliefs, as well they must change their beliefs and intentions in the light of experience. To enable teachers to make these changes reasonably is a central concern of teacher education. My proposed outline of a teacher education program takes as its focus the development of practical reasoning in this sense; indeed, this focus is consistent with as notable an attempt to reform teacher education as the Holmes Report. Whether my proposal will be successful in this is a question that I cannot answer. Surely, though, this must be the focus of any teacher education program; it is the core of what we mean when we talk of translating theory into practice.

Notes

Chapter 1 Introduction

1 Lawrence A. Cremin, *The Education of the Educating Professions* (Washington, D.C.: The American Association of Colleges for Teacher Education, 1977), pp. 12–13.
2 Thomas S. Popkewitz, "Ideology and Social Formation in Teacher Education" in T. S. Popkewitz (ed.), *Critical Studies in Teacher Education: Its Folklore, Theory and Practice* (Philadelphia: The Falmer Press, 1987), p. 17.
3 See, for example, Pierre Bourdieu, *Outline of a Theory of Practice* (Cambridge: Cambridge University Press, 1977).
4 The sources and references for these positions and others mentioned in this chapter will be given in the chapters where the positions are considered in detail.

Chapter 2 Practice as applied science

1 D. J. O'Connor, "The Nature and Scope of Educational Theory" in Glenn Langford and D. J. O'Connor (ed.), *New Essays in the Philosophy of Education* (London: Routledge and Kegan Paul, 1973), pp. 47–65.
2 Ibid., p. 50.
3 See ibid., p. 60.
4 Ibid., p. 60.
5 See John Passmore, *The Philosophy of Teaching* (Cambridge, MA: Harvard University Press, 1980), pp. 87–88.
6 A classic statement of this view is Peter Winch, *The Idea of a Social Science* (London: Routledge and Kegan Paul, 1958).
7 Donald Davidson, "Mental Events" in *Essays on Actions and Events* (Oxford: Oxford University Press, 1982), p. 210.
8 Ibid.
9 Ibid., p. 216.
10 Ibid., p. 222.
11 To allow for probabilistic lawlike statements, one could add to this sentence the clause, "or if one event occurs the other is expected to occur with a specified degree of probability," I will ignore the complications created by probability claims; I do not think the point depends on it.

12 Ernest Hilgard, *Theories of Learning,* second edition (New York: Appleton-Century-Crofts, 1956), p. 486.
13 The Ministry of Education in Nicaragua has published a "Philosophy Program" for teacher training which says, "Our education has as its objective the training of new generations in the scientific, political, ideological and moral principles enunciated by our national leadership, the FSLN (the Sandanista party initials), turning them into convictions and habits of daily life." Quoted in "New Values in Nicaragua," *Manchester Guardian Weekly,* September 8, 1985.
14 Jere Brophy, "Research on Teaching and Teacher Education: The Interface," in Peter Grimmett (ed.), *Research in Teacher Education: Current Problems and Future Prospects in Canada,* (Vancouver: The Centre for the Study of Teacher Education, University of British Columbia, 1984), pp. 78–80.
15 Ibid., p. 78.
16 Ibid.
17 Ibid., p. 79.
18 For an interesting exposition and criticism of this position, see Kieran Egan, *Education and Psychology: Plato, Piaget and Scientific Psychology* (New York: Teachers College Press, 1983), Chapter 3.
19 This discussion is based on an argument developed by Egan in *Education and Psychology,* pp. 134–139.
20 The nature of the indirect relation is my topic in Chapter 7, pp. 106–126.
21 N. L. Gage, *The Scientific Base for the Art of Teaching* (New York: Teachers College Press, 1978).
22 Ibid., p. 15.
23 Ibid., p. 16.
24 Ibid., p. 17.
25 Ibid., p. 18.
26 Ibid., p. 17.
27 Ibid., p. 20.
28 Ibid., p. 20.
29 Ibid., p. 41.
30 Ibid., p. 38.
31 Ibid., p. 39.
32 Ibid.
33 Brophy, op. cit., p. 91.
34 Ibid., p. 82.
35 Ibid., pp. 82–83.
36 Ibid., p. 91.

Chapter 3   An epistemology of practice

1 Donald A. Schön, *The Reflective Practitioner* (New York: Basic Books, 1983). The discussion here is based primarily on Chapter 2. His *Educating*

the Reflective Practitioner (San Francisco: Jossey-Bass, 1987) adds much to his position.

2 *The Reflective Practitioner,* p. 23.
3 Ibid., p. 138. Emphasis in the original.
4 It is possible for Spot and Rover to be category words. I might see a dog that looks like Rover and say that I see it as Rover. I cannot see Rover and say I see it as Rover.
5 *The Reflective Practitioner,* p. 184.
6 Ibid., p. 145.
7 Ibid., p. 147.
8 Ibid., p. 149.
9 See ibid., Chapters 3 and 4.
10 The insulation of science from everyday life is discussed by Thomas S. Kuhn, *The Structure of Scientific Revolutions,* second edition (Chicago: University of Chicago Press, 1970), p. 164.

Chapter 4   Normative theory of education

1 Paul Hirst, "Educational Theory" in J. W. Tibble (ed.), *The Study of Education,* (London: Routledge and Kegan Paul, 1966), pp. 29–58; "The Nature and Scope of Educational Theory (2)" in G. Langford and D. J. O'Connor (eds.), *New Essays in the Philosophy of Education* (London: Routledge and Kegan Paul, 1973), pp. 66–75; "Educational Theory" in Paul Hirst (ed.), *Educational Theory and its Foundation Disciplines* (London: Routledge and Kegan Paul, 1983), pp. 3–29.
2 Paul Hirst, "Educational Theory" in P. H. Hirst (ed.), *Educational Theory and its Foundation Disciplines,* (London: Routledge and Kegan Paul, 1983), p. 3.
3 Ibid., p. 5.
4 Ibid.
5 Hirst develops this view of disciplines in "Liberal Education and the Nature of Knowledge" in *Knowledge and the Curriculum,* (London: Routledge and Kegan Paul, 1974), pp. 30–53.
6 P. H. Hirst, 1983, p. 16.
7 Ibid.
8 Ibid., p. 17.
9 Ibid., p. 18.
10 Ibid., p. 19.
11 Ibid., p. 20.
12 Ibid.
13 Ibid., p. 19.
14 Ibid., p. 20.
15 Ibid.
16 Another account of being "rationally defensible" forms the core of Chapter 7.

Chapter 5 Theory of practice

1 Donna H. Kerr, "The Structure of Quality in Teaching" in Jonas Soltis (ed.), *Philosophy and Education,* National Society for the Study of Education, 76th Yearbook, Part 1, (Bloomington, 1980).
2 Ibid., p. 76.
3 Ibid., p. 76.
4 Ibid., p. 77.
5 Ibid., pp. 77–78.
6 Ibid., p. 76.
7 Ibid., p. 73.
8 Ibid., p. 81.
9 Ibid., p. 62.
10 This use of "conceptual analysis" will be discussed in detail in Chapter 7.

Chapter 6 The nature of teaching

1 On the difficulties in defining the word, "teach," see John Passmore, *The Philosophy of Teaching,* (Cambridge, MA: Harvard University Press, 1980), pp. 19–21.
2 This is, of course, explicitly recognized by Hirst and Kerr. See Chapters 4 and 5.
3 This discussion is suggested by, and adapted from, some ideas of Frederick Olafson, *The Dialectic of Action* (Chicago: University of Chicago Press, 1979), pp. 38–58.
4 These difficulties are adapted from Olafson, op. cit., pp. 52–58, who introduces them in a quite different context.
5 I have tried to describe such a case in "Teaching and Rationality: The Case of Jim Keegstra", *The Journal of Educational Thought,* Vol. 20, No. 1 (April 1986), pp. 1–7.
6 This notion that being a student is closely related to an analysis of teaching is also reached, by a somewhat different route, by Gary Fenstermacher in "Philosophy of Research on Teaching: Three Aspects" in Merlin C. Wittrock (ed.), *Handbook of Research on Teaching,* third edition (New York: Macmillan, 1986), pp. 37–49. Fenstermacher introduces the terms "studenting" and "pupiling" to capture the idea of what one does as a student. "Student" is an American usage; "pupil" is British. Canadians, as is typical, use both. My fifth grade teacher made the distinction this way: "Students study, pupils pupe." Following her, I will use "student."
7 cf. Fenstermacher, p. 39.
8 Annette Baier, "Trust and Antitrust" *Ethics,* Vol. 96. (1986), pp. 231–260.
9 Ibid., p. 232.
10 Ibid., p. 235.
11 Ibid., p. 239.
12 Ibid., pp. 240–241.

13   Ibid., pp. 241–244.

14   Ibid., p. 241.

15   Ibid., p. 242.

16   I want to emphasize that this is one criterion of success in teaching. There can be, and I think are, other criteria for success in teaching. It does make sense to describe a person as a successful teacher even if the students do not learn what is being taught. The criteria of success appealed to in such cases may include such things as the use of the appropriate or desired teaching procedures.

17   This point is noted and clearly presented in David P. Ericson and Frederick S. Ellett, Jr., "Teacher Accountability and the Causal Theory of Teaching," *Educational Theory,* Vol. 37, No. 3 (1987), p. 286.

18   Fenstermacher, op. cit., p. 39.

19   Ibid., pp. 38–39. Emphasis in the original.

20   As Rosy Ruiz so painfully learned. She was the person who crossed the finish line first in the New York Marathon a number of years ago, but was discovered to have travelled by bus for part of the race and was disqualified. You can't win a race unless you have run it.

21   Ibid., p. 39.

22   Thomas F. Green, *The Activities of Teaching* (New York: McGraw-Hill, 1971), p. 140. Emphasis in original.

23   Ibid., p. 141.

24   J. L. Mackie, *The Cement of the Universe* (Oxford: Clarendon Press, 1974), p. 4.

25   The discussion here is drawn from Ericson and Ellett, op. cit., pp. 288–290.

26   The Inus condition is developed by Mackie, op. cit., Chapter 3. It is used by Ericson and Ellett, op. cit. I will ignore the latter's modification to include Inup conditions. That this omission is justified, I hope, will become clear eventually.

27   Mackie, op. cit., p. 62.

28   See for example, Robert Ennis, "On Causality," *Educational Researcher,* Vol. 2, No. 6 (1973), pp. 4–11.

29   H. L. A. Hart and A. M. Honoré, *Causation in the Law* (Oxford: Oxford University Press, 1959), p. 33.

Chapter 7   The practice of teaching

1   Alasdair MacIntyre, *After Virtue,* second edition (Notre Dame, Indiana: University of Notre Dame Press, 1984), p. 187.

2   Ibid., p. 190.

3   Ibid., p. 188.

4   Ibid., pp. 188–189.

5   Ibid., p. 188.

6   "That all human beings teach is in many ways the most important fact about

them." John Passmore, *The Philosophy of Teaching* (Cambridge: Harvard University Press, 1980), p. 25.

7 For a nice account of various views of the purposes of teaching, see Gary Fenstermacher and Jonas Soltis, *Approaches to Teaching* (New York: Teachers College Press, 1986).

8 See Max Black, "Rules and Routines" in R. S. Peters (ed.), *The Concept of Education* (London: Routledge and Kegan Paul, 1967), pp. 92–104.

9 Jere Brophy and Thomas L. Good, "Teacher Behavior and Student Achievement" in Merlin C. Wittrock (ed.), *Handbook of Research on Teaching*, third edition (New York: Macmillan, 1986), p. 341.

10 Richard J. Shavelson and Paula Stern, "Research on Teachers' Pedagogical Thoughts, Judgments, Decisions, and Behavior," *Review of Educational Research*, Vol. 51, No. 4 (Winter, 1981), pp. 455–498.

11 Ibid., p. 478.

12 Ibid., pp. 461–462.

13 Ibid., p. 468.

14 Donald Schön, *The Reflective Practitioner* (New York: Basic Books, 1983), Chapter 2.

15 Erwin Miklos and Myrna L. Greene, "Assessments by Teachers of their Preservice Preparation Programs," *The Alberta Journal of Educational Research*, Vol. 33, No. 3 (September 1987), pp. 191–205.

16 A recent, interesting and controversial example is E. D. Hirsch, Jr., *Cultural Literacy: What Every American Needs to Know* (Boston: Houghton Mifflin, 1987).

17 Intentions and plans are being treated as independent here. It will become clear that in fact they are not independent.

18 Gary D. Fenstermacher, "Philosophy of Research on Teaching: Three Aspects," in Melvin C. Wittrock (ed.), *Handbook of Research on Teaching*, third edition (New York: Macmillan, 1986), p. 44.

19 For example, see I. Wilkinson, J. L. Wardrop and R. C. Anderson, "Silent Reading Reconsidered: Reinterpreting Reading Instruction and Its Effects," *American Educational Research Journal* Vol. 25, No. 1 (Spring 1988) pp. 127–144. To quote from the abstract of this article, "When entry-level abilities were more adequately controlled, silent reading no longer showed a significant effect on post test reading performance. Under alternative models of the data, there is even the suggestion that time spent in oral reading had more effect on final reading achievement." One set of research, combined with certain normative beliefs, suggested the practice of engaging students in silent reading; this research suggests the practice of oral reading. Clearly teachers and teacher educators following this research will need to revise their beliefs; they cannot consistently believe both. Examples such as this, of this point, are easy to find.

20 Gilbert Harman, *Change in View: Principles of Reasoning* (Cambridge, MA: The MIT Press, 1986).

21 Ibid., p. 1.

22 Ibid., p. 29.
23 Ibid.
24 Ibid., p. 30.
25 Ibid., p. 12.
26 Ibid., p. 42.
27 Ibid., p. 32.
28 See ibid., pp. 35–37.
29 Ibid., p. 39.
30 Ibid. A foundational or basic belief would have an intrinsic justification; any other belief, which would be justified by being shown to depend on other, justified beliefs, would have an extrinsic justification.
31 Ibid., p. 115.
32 Ibid., p. 11.
33 Ibid., p. 115.
34 Ibid., p. 6.
35 Ibid., pp. 25–27. It is this kind of explosion that is at the base of my decision to ignore probablistic accounts of causation in Chapter 6.
36 Ibid., pp. 50–51.
37 Ibid., p. 51.
38 Ibid., pp. 52–53.
39 Ibid., p. 68.
40 Ibid., p. 46.
41 Ibid., p. 55.
42 Ibid.
43 Ibid., p. 116.
44 Ibid., p. 56.
45 Ibid., p. 75.
46 Ibid., p. 67.
47 Ibid., p. 67.
48 For some of the issues here see Gilbert Harman, *Thought* (Princeton: Princeton University Press, 1973), pp. 158–161.
49 Harman, *Change in View*, p. 68.
50 See ibid., pp. 80–82, for a discussion of positive and negative intentions.
51 Ibid., p. 77.
52 Ibid., p. 77.
53 Ibid., p. 77.
54 I heard it on CBC Radio, "Pacific Encounters," July 17, 1988.
55 Harman, op. cit., p. 107.
56 See Ralph H. Johnson, "Critical Notice: Gilbert Harman's Change of View: Principles of Reasoning," *Canadian Journal of Philosophy*, Vol. 18, No. 1 (March 1988) pp. 163–178.

Chapter 8   Teacher education

1 See *Tomorrow's Teachers*, The Holmes Group. (East Lansing, MI: The Holmes Group, 1986), pp. 31–36.

2   For the inspiration for this example, see Frances Fitzgerald, *Cities on a Hill* (New York: Simon & Schuster, 1987), p. 159.

3   This marvelously abstruse bit of trivia was used in Ralph H. Johnson, "Critical Notice: Gilbert Harman's *Change in View: Principles of Reasoning*," *Canadian Journal of Philosophy*, Vol. 18, No. 1 (March 1988), p. 173.

4   The Holmes Group, op. cit., p. 62.

5   See Chapter 7, pp. 102–103.

6   There may be overriding reasons that justify the teaching of falsehoods. See Plato's Allegory of the Metals in *The Republic*.

7   For these and other bases for the teaching of information, see John Passmore, *The Philosophy of Teaching* (Cambridge, MA: Harvard University Press, 1980), pp. 94–104.

8   The notion of the logic of a discipline is considered by Paul Hirst in "Liberal Education and the Nature of Knowledge" in his *Knowledge and the Curriculum* (London: Routledge and Kegan Paul, 1974), pp. 30–53, and in his many subsequent essays on the topic.

9   John Passmore, op. cit., p. 60. His distinction between "from experience" and "through experience" is stipulative and interesting. For my purposes here, though, it does not matter; the kind of knowledge at issue here cannot be learned through experience.

10 For more on this sense of "practice," see V. A. Howard, *Artistry* (Indianapolis: Hackett Publishing Company, 1982), Chapter 6.

11 This point is suggested by Passmore, op. cit., p. 28. See also, Israel Scheffler, *Reason and Teaching* (Indianapolis: Bobbs-Merrill, 1973), p. 108.

12 Donald A. Schön, *Educating the Reflective Practitioner* (San Francisco: Jossey-Bass, 1987), p. 17. Emphasis in the original. Throughout this work Schön provides a detailed account and fascinating examples of professionals working as coaches with students.

13 John Dewey, *John Dewey on Education: Selected Writings* (R. D. Archambault, ed.). (Chicago: University of Chicago Press: 1974), p. 151.

14 The Holmes Group, *Tomorrow's Teachers* (East Lansing, MI: The Holmes Group, 1986).

15 Ibid., p. 24.

16 Ibid., p. 23.

17 Ibid., pp. 16–17.

18 Ibid., p. 46.

19 Ibid., p. 28.

20 Ibid., p. 55.

21 Ibid., p. 57.

Bibliography

Archambault, R. D. (ed.), *John Dewey on Education: Selected Writings,* Chicago, University of Chicago Press, 1974.

Baier, A., "Trust and antitrust," *Ethics,* Vol. 96, 1986.

Black, M., "Rules and routines," in R. S. Peters (ed.), *The Concept of Education,* London, Routledge and Kegan Paul, 1967.

Bourdieu, P., *Outline of a Theory of Practice,* Cambridge, Cambridge University Press, 1977.

Brophy, J., "Research on teaching and teacher education: the interface," in P. Grimmett (ed.), *Research in Teacher Education: Current Problems and Future Prospects in Canada,* Vancouver, The Centre for the Study of Teacher Education, University of British Columbia, 1984.

Brophy, J. and Good, T. L., "Teaching behavior and student achievement," in M. C. Wittrock (ed.), *Handbook of Research on Teaching,* third edition, New York, Macmillan, 1986.

Cremin, L. A., *The Education of the Educating Professions,* Washington, D.C., The American Association of Colleges for Teacher Education, 1977.

Davidson, D., "Mental events" in *Essays on Actions and Events,* Oxford, Oxford University Press, 1982.

Egan, K., *Education and Psychology: Plato, Piaget and Scientific Psychology,* New York, Teachers College Press, 1983.

Ennis, R. H., "On causality," *Educational Researcher,* Vol. 2, no. 6, 1973.

Ericson, D. P. and Ellett, F. S., "Teacher accountability and the causal theory of teaching," *Educational Theory,* Vol. 37, no. 3, 1987.

Fenstermacher, G., "Philosophy of research on teaching: three aspects," in M. C. Wittrock (ed.), *Handbook of Research on Teaching,* third edition, New York, Macmillan, 1986.

Fenstermacher, G. and Soltis, J., *Approaches to Teaching,* New York, Teachers College Press, 1986.

Fitzgerald, F., *Cities on a Hill,* New York, Simon and Schuster, 1987.

Gage, N. L., *The Scientific Base for the Art of Teaching,* New York, Teachers College Press, 1978.

Green, T. F., *The Activities of Teaching,* New York, McGraw-Hill, 1971.

Harman, G., *Thought,* Princeton, Princeton University Press, 1973.

Harman, G., *Changes in View: Principles of Reasoning,* Cambridge, The MIT Press, 1986.

Hart, H. L. A. and Honoré, A. M., *Causation in the Law,* Oxford, Oxford University Press, 1959.

Hilgard, E., *Theories of Learning,* second edition, New York, Appleton-Century-Crofts, 1956.

Hirsch, E. D., Jr., *Cultural Literacy: What Every American Needs to Know,* Boston, Houghton Mifflin, 1987.

Hirst, P. H., "Educational theory," in J. W. Tibble (ed.), *The Study of Education,* London, Routledge and Kegan Paul, 1966.

Hirst, P. H. "Educational theory," in P. H. Hirst (ed.), *Educational Theory and its Foundation Disciplines,* London, Routledge and Kegan Paul, 1983.

Hirst, P. H., "The nature and scope of educational theory (2)" in G. Langford and D. J. O'Connor (eds.), *New Essays in the Philosophy of Education,* London, Routledge and Kegan Paul, 1973.

Hirst, P. H. "Liberal education and the nature of knowledge," in P. H. Hirst (ed.), *Knowledge and the Curriculum,* London, Routledge and Kegan Paul, 1974.

Holmes Group, The, *Tomorrow's Teachers,* East Lansing, MI, The Holmes Group, 1986.

Howard, V. A., *Artistry,* Indianapolis, Hackett Publishing Company, 1982.

Johnson, R. H., "Critical notice of Gilbert Harman *Changes in View: Principles of Reasoning,*" *Canadian Journal of Philosophy,* Vol. 18, no. 1, 1988.

Kerr, D. H., "The structure of quality in teaching," in J. Soltis (ed.), *Philosophy and Education,* Bloomington, IN, National Society for the Study of Education, 76th yearbook, Part 1, 1980.

Kuhn, T. S., *The Structure of Scientific Revolutions,* second edition, Chicago, University of Chicago Press, 1970.

MacIntyre, A., *After Virtue,* second edition, Notre Dame, IN, University of Notre Dame Press, 1984.

Mackie, J. L., *The Cement of the Universe,* Oxford, Clarendon Press, 1974.

Miklos, E. and Green, M. L., "Assessments by teachers of their preservice preparation programs," *Alberta Journal of Educational Research,* Vol. 33, no. 3, 1987.

O'Connor, D. J., "The nature and scope of educational theory," in G. Langford and D. J. O'Connor (eds.), *New Essays in Philosophy of Education,* London, Routledge and Kegan Paul, 1973.

Olafson, F., *The Dialectic of Action,* Chicago, University of Chicago Press, 1979.

Passmore, J., *The Philosophy of Teaching,* Cambridge, Harvard University Press, 1980.

Pearson, A. T., "Teaching and rationality: the case of Jim Keegstra," *Journal of Educational Thought,* Vol. 20, no. 1, 1986.

Popkewitz, T. S., "Ideology and social formation in teacher education," in T. S. Popkewitz (ed.), *Critical Studies in Teacher Education: Its Folklore, Theory and Practice,* Philadelphia, The Falmer Press, 1987.

Scheffler, I., *Reason and Teaching,* Indianapolis, Bobbs-Merrill, 1973.

Schön, D. A., *The Reflective Practitioner,* New York, Basic Books, 1983.

Schön, D. A., *Educating the Reflective Practitioner,* San Francisco, Jossey-Bass, 1987.

Shavelson, R. J. and Stern, P., "Research on teachers' pedagogical thoughts, judgments, decisions and behavior," *Review of Educational Research,* Vol. 51, no. 4, 1981.

Wilkinson, I., Wardrop, J. L., and Anderson, R. C., "Silent reading reconsidered: reinterpreting reading and its effects," *American Educational Research Journal,* Vol. 25, no. 1, 1988.

Winch, P., *The Idea of a Social Science,* London, Routledge and Kegan Paul, 1958.

Index

370.71 P361t

Pearson, Allen T., 1944-

The teacher : theory and
practice in teacher
1989.

DATE